**TRAINS and
BOATS and
PLANES and . . .**

TRAINS and BOATS and PLANES and...

CUSTOM-BUILDING WOODEN TOYS

C. J. MAGINLEY

Illustrated by Elisabeth D. McKee

Photographs by Joseph J. Moffa

HAWTHORN BOOKS, INC.
Publishers/New York
A Howard & Wyndham Company

For Ruth S. Maginley

Contents

Acknowledgments

My sincere thanks to three people who made this book possible.

To Elisabeth D. McKee for her many hours of painstaking work preparing the illustrations and for all the suggestions and assistance which she gave me.

To Ruth S. Maginley for her accurate translation of my handwriting into a readable manuscript with her typewriter.

To Joseph J. Moffa for the interest and care which he took in photographing the toys.

**TRAINS and
BOATS and
PLANES and . . .**

Introduction

Making wooden toys is fun and you can gain a great deal of satisfaction by making a toy of which you can be proud. The toy will be a prized possession of the child to whom it is given because it has been made by someone he knows.

Many have found that there is a good market for well-made wooden toys and supplement their income in this way. Craft shows, of which there are many, are one of the best outlets for handcrafted toys.

Soon after making some of the toys described in this book, you will find yourself making changes or creating designs of your own. Nothing is more gratifying to a craftsman than to admire an object he has made with his own hands.

The actual dimensions of the pieces of wood being used are given in this book. When purchasing material at the lumberyard, you will find that a piece 3/4″ × 5 1/2″, for example, is called a 1 × 6.

The widths of lumber may vary somewhat. A 1 × 6 may be 3/4″ × 5 5/8″ or 3/4″ × 5 1/2″. At the present time it is much likelier to be 5 1/2″. Hopefully, it will not get any narrower.

The following table gives the nominal size and the actual size:

Nominal Size	Actual Size
1 × 2	3/4″ × 1 5/8″ or 1 1/2″
1 × 4	3/4″ × 3 5/8″ or 3 1/2″
1 × 6	3/4″ × 5 1/2″
1 × 8	3/4″ × 7 1/2″
1/2 × 4	7/16″ × 3 1/2″
1/2 × 6	7/16″ × 5 1/2″

The thickness is always given first, so when a dimension such as 7/16″ × 2″ × 3″ is given, it means that the piece is 7/16″ thick, 2″ wide, and 3″ long.

Whenever possible each toy has been made in proportion to the actual object (truck, automobile, etc.). However, it has not been practical to make all of the toys in a set to the same scale.

As toys, they must be neither too large nor too small. For example, the monoplane and tow tractors and trailers, if made to the same scale as the jet, would be too small to be practical. The toy must be large enough and sturdy enough for a child to play with.

Any of the toys can be made larger or smaller by changing some dimensions of the materials used. The steps in the construction would be practically the same. As one example, the open-top trailer truck and tractor could be enlarged by multiplying most dimensions by 1 1/2. Or, the ambulance could be made larger to correspond in size to the large fire engines by making it the size of the delivery van (page 23).

If the open-top trailer and tractor are enlarged, the new dimensions for the tractor would be approximately as follows:

1 piece 3/4″ × 2 1/4″ × 9″——frame
1 piece 1 3/4″ × 3 3/8″ × 4 1/8″——A $\Big\}$ cab and engine
1 piece 1 1/8″ × 3 3/8″ × 2 3/4″——B
1 piece 3/8″ × 3/4″ × 3 3/4″——bumper
1 piece 3/16″ × 1 1/2″ × 1 1/2″——fifth wheel
1 piece 3/4″ × 1 1/8″ × 2 1/4″——front $\Big\}$ axle holders
1 piece 3/4″ × 3 1/2″ × 2 1/4″——rear

These new dimensions are not in all cases exactly 1 1/2 times those given as it is more convenient to use only standard thicknesses of wood, namely 7/16″, 3/4″, 1 1/8″, and 1 3/4″. For a truck as large as this one would be, a 2″ wheel is desirable, so the rear axle holder would have to be more than 1 1/2 times as wide. The axle lengths would depend on the thickness of the wheels used.

The enlarged dimensions for the trailer would be approximately as follows:

1 piece 7/16″ × 3 1/2″ × 13 1/2″——bottom
2 pieces 3/4″ × 2 1/4″ × 2 5/8″——ends
2 pieces 7/16″ × 2 1/4″ × 13 1/2″——sides
2 pieces 3/4″ × 1 3/4″ × 2 1/4″——x $\Big\}$ axle holders
1 piece 3/4″ × 1 1/2″ × 2 1/4″——y

The 7/16″ material for the bottom is adequate and need not be changed. Also 7/16″ stock is to be used for the sides instead of 3/8″. When larger toys are made it will be necessary to fasten some of the parts together with nails, screws, or dowels in addition to the glue. The sides and bottom of the trailer, for example, should be nailed or doweled to the ends. In short, make your own adjustments as needed to obtain the desired result with larger or smaller toys.

SOME SUGGESTIONS • MATERIALS

Clear pine, basswood, and poplar are all good for making toys and are easier to work with than hardwoods such as birch or maple.

Plywood in sizes of 1/8″, 3/16″, or 1/4″ is very good for making many of the parts listed.

It is often possible to obtain good pieces of scrap wood at a woodworking shop. Take advantage of this source, if available.

When a thicker or wider piece is needed, two or more pieces can be glued together to obtain the desired result.

Hardwood, such as birch or maple, should be used for bumpers.

Axle lengths may vary from those given due to the thickness of the wheels being used. The axle lengths given for each toy assume that the 1″ wheels are 1/4″ thick; the 1 1/4″ wheels are 3/8″; the 1 1/2″ wheels are 7/16″; and the 2″ wheels are 1/2″ thick.

The diameter of dowels may vary and adjustments will have to be made. It is a good idea to have drill bits a little larger or smaller than the dowels being used.

Pieces of dowel or axle pegs can be used for headlights in place of the furniture nails.

Applicator sticks that are 3/32″ dowels can be obtained at some drugstores.

Beads can be purchased at stores that sell craft supplies.

4

MORE SUGGESTIONS

Read the directions, study the photograph and drawings before starting to make a toy.

The directions assume that you will use power tools.

All the toys can be made with a circular saw, belt-disc sander, and drill press. A planer blade and a fine-tooth crosscut blade for the saw will save a lot of sanding.

The toys described in this book are glued together. Cover the parts to be joined with a thin coat of glue spread evenly over the entire surface of one or both parts. All of the white glues are very good, as are Titebond and Elmer's Carpenter's glue. In most cases no clamping is necessary. When making boxes for the trucks and trains, strong rubber bands will provide enough pressure to ensure a good bond.

Each part of a toy should be sanded before assembly. The completed toy should be thoroughly sanded and all sharp edges eliminated.

Production paper is better for sanding than regular sandpaper.

A piece of small dowel, a round toothpick, or an applicator stick can be inserted into a hole in a coupler bar to ensure that the dowel hitch does not come out.

The location of a hole is measured from the center of the hole.

Headlights may be recessed by drilling a hole slightly larger than the head of the furniture nail or axle pin.

Wooden axles are used for all the wheeled toys in this book. By making a few changes, the dowel axles can be replaced with screws. No. 6 or no. 8 roundhead screws are very satisfactory.

When mounting double wheels, as on the trucks, drill a slightly larger hole through the inside wheel so that it will turn freely on the axle. The hole in the outside wheel may be slightly smaller than the dowel axle to provide a tight fit.

The finish should be applied to a toy before the wheels are put on. A sanding sealer and one or two coats of varnish will give a very satisfactory finish. When the sealer is dry it should be lightly sanded with no. 220 production paper, after which one or two coats of satin varnish are applied.

There are several polyurethane varnishes that are also very good. Any finish used must be nontoxic.

A WORD ABOUT WHEELS

A well-designed and carefully made toy deserves to have good wheels. The wheels are a vital part of a toy if it is to function satisfactorily. Sources where wheels can be purchased are listed in the appendix. I believe that you will be better satisfied with your creations if you use commercially made wheels.

Of course, if a lathe is available, you can make good wheels; when only a few wheels are needed, this is a most satisfactory method.

Wheels can be made on the drill press, running at a slow speed, with a hole saw. Or a single-wing circle cutter can be used. In either case, the material for the wheels should be clamped to a wooden facing fastened to the drill-press table. When using the circle cutter or hole saw, cut part way through the stock, turn it over and finish from that side. Sand all of the edges.

MAKING AXLE HOLDERS

For the wheeled toys, axle holders will be needed to allow the axles to turn freely in them. Refer back to the directions here for the construction of the axle holders for each toy. They are similar in construction and vary only in size and diameter of the hole for the axle, which are given for each toy. The length of the axles may differ somewhat from that listed due to the

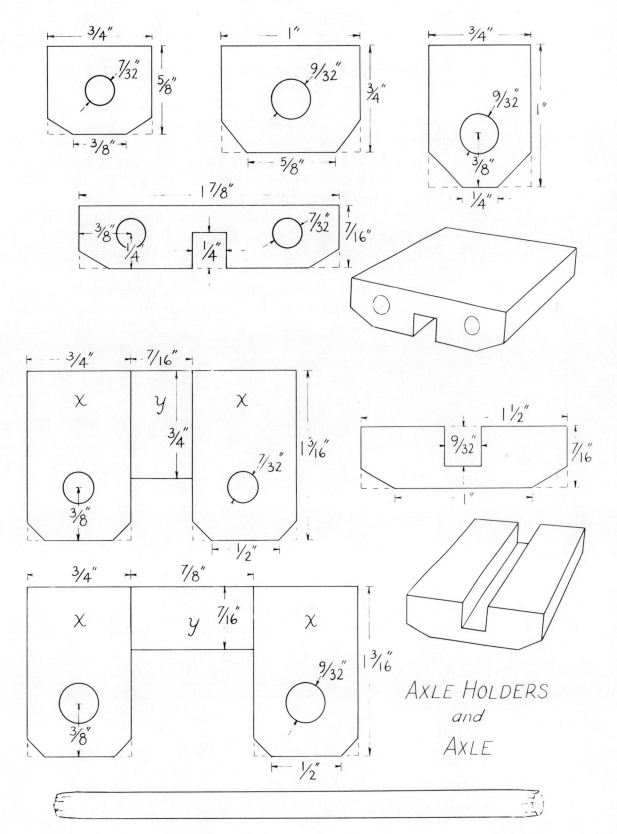

3/4"
7/32"
5/8"
3/8"

1"
9/32"
3/4"
5/8"

3/4"
9/32"
1"
3/8"
1/4"

1 7/8"
3/8"
1/4"
1/4"
7/32"
7/16"

3/4"
7/16"
x
y
x
3/4"
7/32"
1 3/16"
3/8"
1/2"

1 1/2"
9/32"
7/16"
1"

3/4"
7/8"
x
y
7/16"
x
1 3/16"
9/32"
3/8"
1/2"

AXLE HOLDERS
and
AXLE

thickness of the wheels used, so some minor adjustments in measurements may have to be made.

While not necessary, the holders do look better when the lower side edges are sawed off at about a 30-degree angle as shown in the diagram.

When cutting a 9/32″ × 9/32″ groove, be sure that the dowel axle will revolve easily in the groove when the axle holder is glued to the frame.

When making the double axle holders for the trailers, the y piece is glued between the two x pieces.

Put wax on the axles or spray them with silicone to make the toy run better.

Dents made by pinching the ends of the axles with pliers will result in a better bond between the wheel and axle when glue is applied.

1
On City & Suburban Streets

Compact Auto

Hatchback Auto

Fuel Oil Truck

Moving Van

Garbage Truck

Parcel Delivery Truck

Delivery Van

Lumber Truck

Service Station

Included in this set are the trucks most commonly seen around the city and suburbs. These are the vehicles that service the stores, factories, and homes in the community. It would be difficult to imagine life in urban areas without these trucks. It goes without saying that cars are an integral part of the street scene as well, and the two models given here add diversity to that scene as reproduced through the toymaker's craft.

COMPACT AUTO

Materials

    1 piece 3/4″ × 1 5/8″ × 4 5/8″——body
    1 piece 7/16″ × 1 9/16″ × 2″——roof
    2 small furniture nails——headlights
    2 pieces 3/16″ dowel 2 1/4″ long——axles
    4   1″ wheels

Construction

1. 3/4″ from each end of the body, drill 7/32″ holes for the axles 1/4″ up from the lower edge.

2. Round off the upper front and rear edges and sand the surface.

3. Saw each end of the roof with the saw set at 40 degrees. Saw along each side with a 5-degree setting.

4. Glue the roof to the body 2″ from the front end.

5. Drive in the headlights 1/2″ from the lower edge and 1/4″ from the side edges.

Front View

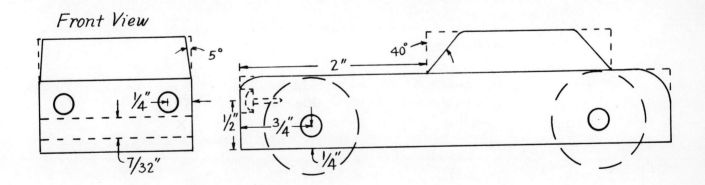

HATCHBACK AUTO

Materials

2 pieces 3/4″ × 1″ × 5 1/2″——A
1 piece 7/16″ × 1″ × 5 1/2″——B $\Big\}$ body
1 piece 7/16″ × 1 7/8″ × 3 1/2″——roof
2 pieces 3/16″ × 3/8″ × 2 1/8″——bumpers——hardwood
2 small furniture nails——headlights
2 pieces 3/16″ dowel 2 1/4″ long——axles
4   1″ wheels

Construction

1. Glue the three body pieces together with the 7/16″ piece in the middle. A different color wood, such as redwood, walnut, or mahogany, used for the 7/16″ piece makes an interesting contrast when a clear finish is applied.

2. With a 1 1/4″ Greenlee type bit make the wheel wells. Locate the front well 1″ from the end and the rear well 1 1/4″ from the end. The center of each well should be 1/4″ from the lower edge. Drill a 7/32″ hole through the centers of the wells.

3. Round off the upper front edge. Drive in the headlights 1/4″ from the side edges and 5/8″ from the lower edge.

4. Shape the roof as shown in the diagram. Tilt the saw blade at 5 degrees and saw off each side edge. Glue on the roof even with the back end of the body.

5. Glue on the bumpers.

6. A small hole may be drilled in the center of the rear end into which the gasoline pump hose may be inserted.

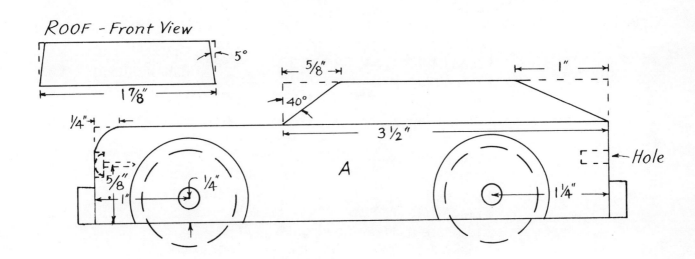

ROOF - Front View

13

FUEL OIL TRUCK

Materials

    1 piece 7/16″ × 1 3/4″ × 10″——frame
    1 piece 1 1/8″ × 2 1/2″ × 3 1/4″——A ⎫
                                        ⎬ cab and hood
    1 piece 3/4″ × 2 1/2″ × 1 1/2″——B ⎭
    2 pieces 3/4″ × 1″ × 1 3/4″——axle holders
    1 piece 1/4″ × 1/2″ × 2 3/4″——bumper—hardwood
    1 piece 1 1/8″ × 3″ × 7″——upper ⎫
    1 piece 3/4″ × 3″ × 7″——lower   ⎬ tank
    2 pieces 1/2″ dowel 1/2″ long——hatch covers ⎭
    1 piece 1/4″ × 1 3/4″ × 7″——tank support
    1 piece 1/4″ × 1″ × 7″——catwalk
    2 furniture nails——headlights
    1 piece 1/4″ dowel 2 3/4″ long——front axle
    1 piece 1/4″ dowel 3 3/8″long——rear axle
    6   1 1/4″ wheels

Construction

1. Round off one edge (front) of the A piece and sand the upper surface. Set the saw at 15 degrees and saw off one edge (front) of the B piece. Glue B to A and round off the back edge of B.

2. Drive in the headlights 3/4″ from the lower edge and 1/4″ from the side edges.

3. Shape the axle holders. See page 7. Drill a 9/32″ hole lengthwise through the center of each.

4. Glue the front holder to the frame 1/4″ from the end and the rear holder 2″ from the end.

5. Glue the cab assembly to the frame letting it extend 3/16″ beyond the end.

6. Round off the ends of the bumper and glue it to the frame.

7. Glue the tank support to the frame and against the cab.

8. Glue the two pieces for the tank together and round off all edges.

9. Glue the catwalk to the center of the top of the tank. Then 2″ from either end of the catwalk drill a 1/2″ hole 3/8″ deep for the hatch covers. Round off the top edges of the covers and insert them into the holes.

10. Glue the tank to the tank support.

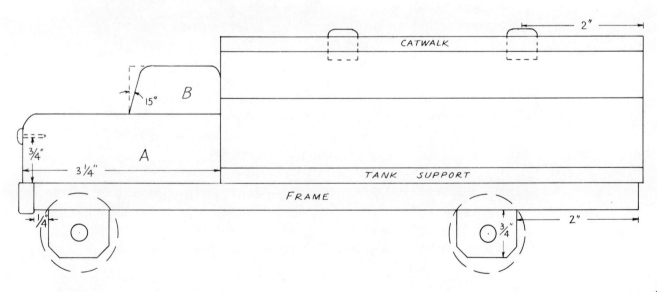

MOVING VAN

Materials

    1 piece 7/16″ × 1 1/2″ × 8 1/2″——frame
    1 piece 1 1/8″ × 2″ × 2 1/4″——A }
    1 piece 7/16″ × 2″ × 1 1/8″——B } engine, cab assembly
    2 pieces 1/4″ × 1 1/2″ × 7″——sides—lower section
    2 pieces 1/4″ × 1″ × 8 1/2″——sides—upper section
    1 piece 7/16″ × 2 1/2″ × 1 7/8″——rear end
    1 piece 7/16″ × 1 1/2″ × 1 7/8″——front end—lower
    1 piece 7/16″ × 1″ × 1 7/8″——front end—upper
    1 piece 1/4″ × 2 3/8″ × 7″——bottom
    1 piece 1/8″ × 2 3/8″ × 1 1/2″——bottom—over cab
    1 piece 1/4″ × 2 3/8″ × 8 1/2″——roof
    2 pieces 1/4″ × 3/4″ × 1 13/16″——C
    1 piece 1/4″ × 1/2″ × 2 1/4″——bumper—hardwood
    2 pieces 5/8″ × 3/4″ × 1 1/2″——axle holders
    1 piece 3/16″ dowel 2 1/8″ long——front axle
    1 piece 3/16″ dowel 2 5/8″ long——rear axle
    6   1″ wheels

Construction

1. Round off one edge (front) of the A piece and sand the upper surface. Saw off one end of the B piece with the saw tilted at 15 degrees. Glue B to A and round off the back edge of B.

2. Install the headlights about 3/4″ from the lower surface of A and 1/4″ from the side edges.

3. Drill a 7/32″ hole lengthwise through the center of each axle holder (see page 7).

4. Glue the front axle holder to the frame 1/4″ from the end and the rear holder 1 3/8″ from the end.

5. Glue the assembled cab to the frame letting it extend 3/16″ beyond the end of the frame.

6. Round off the ends of the bumper and glue it to the end of the frame.

7. Glue the two side sections together (see diagram). Sand the completed sides.

8. Glue the sides to the three end pieces.

9. Attach the two bottom pieces.

10. Glue the C pieces to the underside of the roof, which is removable, 1/2″ from the ends and equidistant from the side edges.

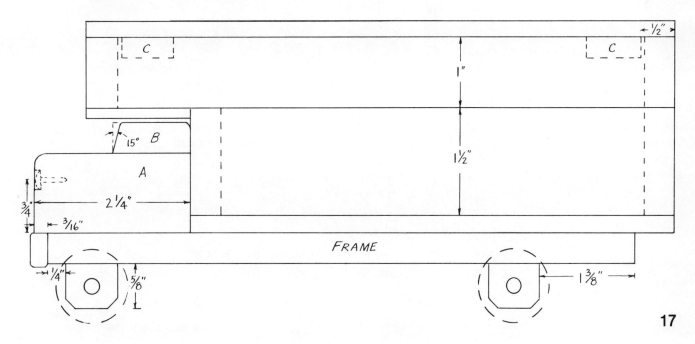

17

GARBAGE TRUCK

Materials

1 piece 7/16″ × 1 3/4″ × 7″——frame
1 piece 1 1/8″ × 2 1/2″ × 2 3/4″——A ⎫
1 piece 3/4″ × 2 1/2″ × 1 3/8″——B ⎬ cab and hood
1 piece 1/4″ × 1/2″ × 2 1/2″——bumper—hardwood
2 pieces 3/4″ × 1″ × 1 3/4″——axle holders
2 furniture nails——headlights
2 pieces 1/4″ × 1 3/4″ × 4 1/2″——sides ⎫
1 piece 7/16″ × 1 3/4″ × 2 1/2″——front end ⎪
1 piece 1/4″ × 3/4″ × 2 1/2″——brace ⎪
1 piece 1/4″ × 3″ × 4 3/4″——floor ⎬ box
1 piece 1/4″ × 3″ × 4″——roof ⎪
1 piece 1/4″ × 1 3/4″ × 1 3/4″——step
1 piece 1/8″ × 1/2″ × 3″——C
1 piece 1/4″ dowel 2 3/4″ long——front axle
1 piece 1/4″ dowel 3 3/8″ long——rear axle
6   1 1/4″ wheels

18

Construction

1. Round off one edge (front) of the A piece. Sand the upper surface. With the saw set at 15 degrees saw off one end of the B piece. Glue B to A and round off the back edge of B.

2. Drive in the headlights 3/4" from the lower edge and 1/4" from the side edges.

3. Make the axle holders (see page 7). Drill a 9/32" hole lengthwise through the center of each.

4. Glue the front holder to the frame 1/2" from the end and the rear holder 1" from the end.

5. Glue the step to the frame against the rear axle holder.

6. Glue the cab to the frame letting it extend 3/16" beyond the end.

7. Round off the ends of the bumper and glue it to the frame.

8. Shape the sides (see diagram). Glue the sides to the end and glue on the floor.

9. Glue the brace to the underside of the roof 1/4" from the end (rear) and equidistant from the side edges. Glue on the roof. Glue the C piece to the ends and floor of the box.

10. Glue the assembled box to the frame and against the cab.

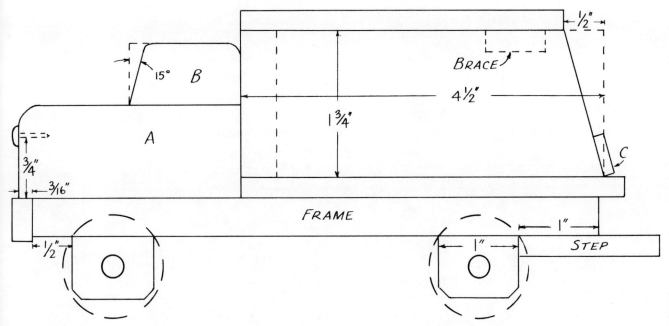

PARCEL DELIVERY TRUCK

Materials

1 piece 7/16″ × 1 1/2″ × 5 1/2″——frame
1 piece 1 1/8″ × 2 3/8″ × 1 1/4″——hood
1 piece 7/16″ × 1 3/4″ × 2 3/8″——dashboard, windshield
1 piece 1/4″ × 1/2″ × 2 1/2″——bumper—hardwood
1 piece 7/16″ × 1 1/2″ × 1 7/8″——back end
1 piece 7/16″ × 1/2″ × 1 7/8″——front end
2 pieces 1/4″ × 1 1/2″ × 3 1/2″——sides
1 piece 1/4″ × 2 3/8″ × 3 1/2″——bottom
1 piece 7/16″ × 2 3/8″ × 5″
1 piece 1/4″ × 1 13/16″ × 2 9/16″——A ⎫ roof
1 piece 1/4″ × 1/2″ × 1/2″——bottom ⎫
1 piece 1/8″ × 1/2″ × 3/4″——back ⎬ seat
1 piece 3/16″ dowel 3/4″ long——seat support ⎭

1 piece 3/16" dowel 1" long——steering wheel shaft
1   3/4" wheel——steering wheel
2 pieces 7/16" × 1/2" × 1 1/4"——steps
2 pieces 5/8" × 3/4" × 1 1/2"——axle holders
2 furniture nails——headlights
1 piece 3/16" dowel 2 1/8" long——front axle
1 piece 3/16" dowel 2 5/8" long——rear axle
6   1" wheels

Construction

1. Round off one edge (front) of the hood. Glue the dashboard and windshield to the end of the hood.

2. Drive in the headlights 3/4" from the lower edge and 1/4" from the side edges.

3. In the dashboard drill a 3/16" hole at an angle downward about 1/2" deep. Locate the hole 3/4" from the left end of the dashboard and 7/8" from the upper edge.

4. Fasten the steering wheel to the shaft and glue the shaft in the hole.

5. Drill a 3/16" hole in the frame 2 1/8" from the front end, 1/4" deep and 5/8" from one edge (left) for the seat support.

6. Make the axle holders (see page 7). Drill a 7/32" hole lengthwise through the center of each. Glue the front holder to the frame 3/8" from the end and the rear holder 5/8" from the end.

7. Glue the hood assembly to the frame letting it extend 3/16" beyond the end.

8. Round off the ends of the bumper and glue it to the frame.

9. Glue the sides of the box to the ends. The 1/2" wide piece or front end should be at the top even with the upper edges of the sides. Glue the bottom on.

10. Round off one end of the roof (front). Glue the A piece to the underside about 1/2" from the rear end.

11. In the center of the seat drill a 3/16" hole about 3/16" in depth. Glue the back on and insert the support into the hole. Install the seat in the frame.

12. Glue the box to the frame 1 ″ back from the dashboard.
13. Rabbet out a piece 1/4 ″ × 1/4 ″ from each step piece. Glue a step to each side of the frame.

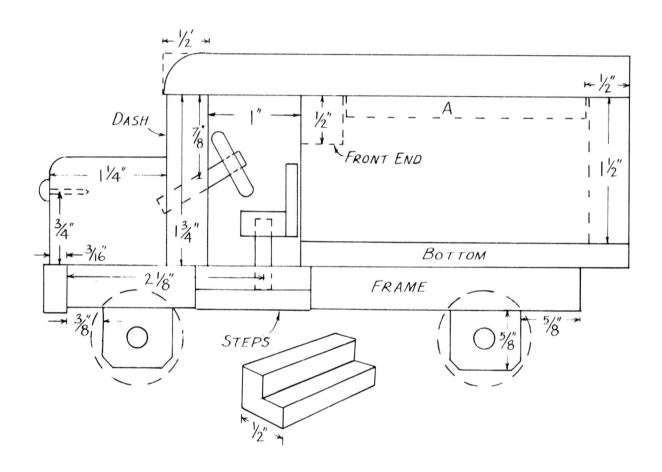

DELIVERY VAN

Materials

   1 piece 7/16″ × 1 3/4″ × 8 1/2″——frame
   1 piece 1 1/8″ × 2 1/2″ × 3 1/4″——A ⎫
   1 piece 3/4″ × 2 1/2″ × 1 1/2″——B   ⎬ cab and hood
   1 piece 1/4″ × 1/2″ × 2 3/4″——bumper—hardwood
   2 pieces 3/4″ × 1″ × 1 3/4″——axle holders
   2 pieces 7/16″ × 2 1/2″ × 2 3/4″——ends   ⎫
   2 pieces 1/4″ × 2 1/2″ × 6″——sides   ⎪
   1 piece 1/4″ × 3 1/4″ × 6″——bottom   ⎬ box
   1 piece 1/4″ × 3 1/4″ × 6″——roof   ⎪
   2 pieces 1/4″ × 3/4″ × 2 11/16″——underpieces ⎭
   2 furniture nails——headlights
   1 piece 1/4″ dowel 2 3/4″ long——front axle
   1 piece 1/4″ dowel 3 3/8″ long——rear axle
   6   1 1/4″ wheels

Construction

1. Round off one edge (front) of the A piece and sand the upper surface.

2. Saw off one end of the B piece with the saw set at 15 degrees.

3. Glue B to A and round off the back edge of B.

4. Drive in the headlights about 1/4″ from the side edges and 3/4″ from the lower surface.

5. Shape the axle holders (see page 7). Drill a 9/32″ hole lengthwise through the center.

6. Glue the front holder to the frame 1/4″ from the end and the rear holder 1″ from the end.

7. Glue the cab assembly to the frame letting it extend 1/4″.

8. Round off the ends of the bumper and glue it to the frame.

9. Glue the sides of the box to the ends and attach the bottom.

10. Glue the underpieces to the roof 1/2″ from the ends and equidistant from the side edges.

11. Glue the box to the frame.

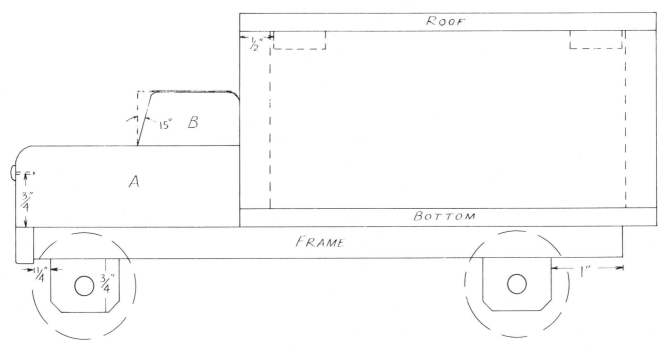

24

LUMBER TRUCK

Materials

    1 piece 7/16″ × 1 3/4″ × 9″——frame
    1 piece 1 1/8″ × 2 1/2″ × 3 1/4″——A ⎫
    1 piece 3/4″ × 2 1/2″ × 1 1/2″——B ⎬ cab and hood
    2 pieces 3/4″ × 1″ × 1 3/4″——axle holders
    1 piece 1/4″ × 1/2″ × 2 3/4″——bumper——hardwood
    1 piece 7/16″ × 3″ × 6 1/4″——platform
    1 piece 7/16″ × 1 3/8″ × 3″——end
    2 furniture nails——headlights
    8 pieces 1/4″ dowel 1 1/2″ long——stakes
    1 piece 1/4″ dowel 2 3/4″ long——front axle
    1 piece 1/4″ dowel 3 3/8″ long——rear axle
    6   1 1/4″ wheels

25

Construction

1. Round off one edge (front) of the A piece and sand the upper surface. With the saw tilted at 15 degrees saw off one end of the B piece. Glue B to A and round off the back edge of B.

2. Drive in the headlights about 3/4" from the lower side and 1/4" from the side edges.

3. Make the axle holders (see page 7). Drill a 9/32" hole lengthwise through the center of each.

4. Glue the front axle holder to the frame 1/4" from the end and the rear holder 1" from the end.

5. Glue the cab assembly to the frame letting it extend about 1/4" beyond the end of the frame.

6. Round off the ends of the bumper and glue it in place.

7. Glue the end piece to the platform and glue the platform to the frame.

8. If stakes are to be installed, drill four 1/4" holes about 5/16" deep along each side 1/4" in from the edges. Space holes 1 1/8" apart starting at the front.

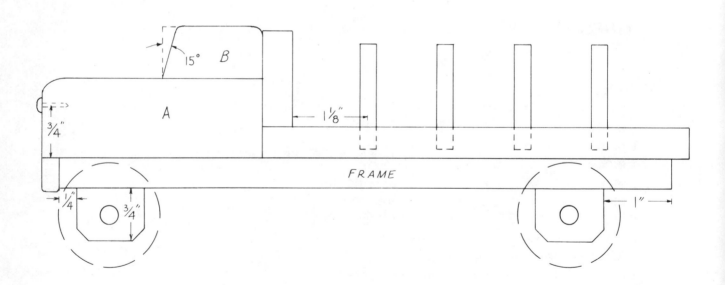

SERVICE STATION

Materials

2 pieces 3/4″ × 3 5/8″ × 8 1/2″——sides
1 piece 3/4″ × 3 5/8″ × 12″——back
2 pieces 3/4″ × 3 5/8″ × 7 3/4″——partitions
1 piece 1/4″ × 9 1/2″ × 13 1/2″——floor—plywood
1 piece 1/4″ × 9 1/4″ × 13 1/2″——roof—plywood
4 pieces 7/16″ × 3/4″ × 3 5/8″——end posts
2 pieces 7/16″ × 3 1/2″ × 3 15/16″——overhead doors
2 pieces 1/4″ dowel 3/4″ long (or use axle pins)——door
    handles
4 pieces 1/4″ × 1 1/8″ × 4 1/4″——door stops
4 pieces 1/4″ × 1/2″ × 3″——tracks
2 pieces 7/16″ × 3/4″ × 3″——sides   ⎫
2 pieces 1/4″ × 3/4″ × 2 1/2″——upper—lower   ⎬ office door assembly
1 piece 7/16″ × 1 1/2″ × 3″——door   ⎭
1 piece 1/4″ dowel 3/4″ long (or use
    axle pin)——knob
6 no. 4   1 1/2″ finishing nails
No. 16   1″ brads
10 no. 6   1 1/2″ flathead screws

27

Construction

1. In one partition, cut a groove the length of the partition about 1/8″ wide, 1/4″ deep, and 1/4″ from the upper edge. The head of a no. 4 finishing nail will slide in this groove. In the partition between the bays cut similar grooves on both sides. In the side piece or outside wall of the left-hand bay cut the same kind of groove along the upper inside surface but only about 5″ long, starting at the front end. To cut this groove it will be necessary to move the fence from 1/4″ away from the blade to 3 3/8″ if the stock is 3 5/8″ wide. Or, the groove can be made the full length of the side, in which case a small opening would be in the back but could be closed with a wood filler.

2. On the outside surface of each side, drill and countersink three holes for screws 3/8″ in from the rear edge. Locate the holes 1/2″ from the upper and lower edges with one in the middle.

3. In the back, drill and countersink holes for screws into the partitions 3/4″ from the top and bottom edges. The holes for the office partition are in 2 7/8″ from the end and those for the bay partition are 4 3/8″ from the other end.

4. Screw the sides to the back and install the partitions. Each bay will be approximately 4″ wide.

5. Nail on the floor, which will extend about 1″ at the front.

6. Glue the stops over the saw cuts, even with the upper edge of the side and partitions and against the back.

7. Glue the tracks to the side and partitions, below the grooves, 5/8″ from the upper edges. The ends of the tracks should be against the stops.

8. Saw off the lower inside edge and upper outside edge of each overhead door. In the front of each door drill a hole about 1/4″ deep and 1/4″ up from the bottom edge and centered for the handles. Drive the no. 4 nails into the ends of each door 1/4″ down from the top edge and centered. The heads should protrude about 3/16″.

9. In each upper and lower frame piece for the office door drill a pilot hole for a no. 4 nail 3/4″ from one end and centered. Drive in the nails.

10. Glue the lower piece to the floor so that the front edge is even with the ends of the partition and side and the nail is 3/4″ from the side.

11. Glue the side frame pieces to the partition, side, and lower frame piece.

12. Saw off the outside right-hand corner of the door and the inside left-hand corner. Drill a hole for the knob 1 1/4″ from the bottom and 1/4″ from the edge.

13. Also, in the door, drill holes in the top and bottom 1/4″ from the right-hand side and centered. These are for the nails on which the door will swing.

14. Set the door in place on the lower nail. Insert the nail, in the upper frame piece, into the hole in the door and glue the upper piece to the side pieces.

15. Slide the overhead doors into the grooves and glue the posts to the ends of the sides and partitions.

16. Nail on the roof which will extend about 1/4″ at the front.

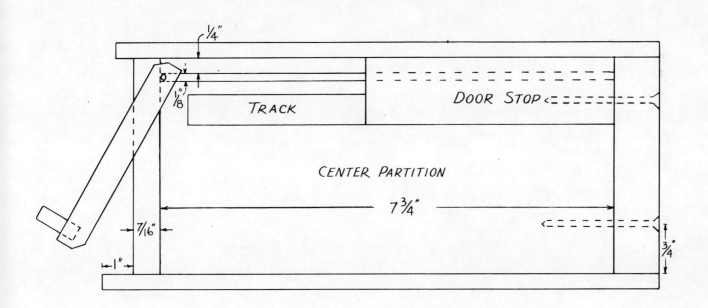

UPPER ENDS OF PARTITIONS

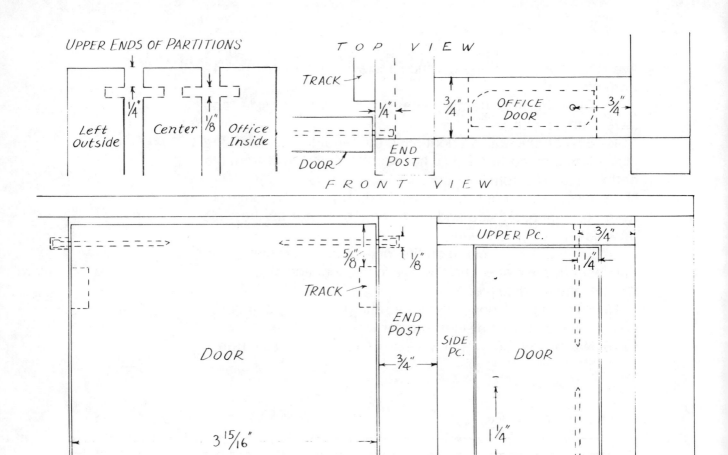

TOP VIEW

TRACK

3/4" OFFICE DOOR 3/4"

1/4"

Left Outside   Center   1/8"   Office Inside

DOOR

END POST

FRONT VIEW

TRACK

5/8"   1/8"

DOOR

END POST

3/4"

UPPER PC.   3/4"

1/4"

SIDE PC.   DOOR

1/4"

3 15/16"

LOWER PC.

BACK VIEW

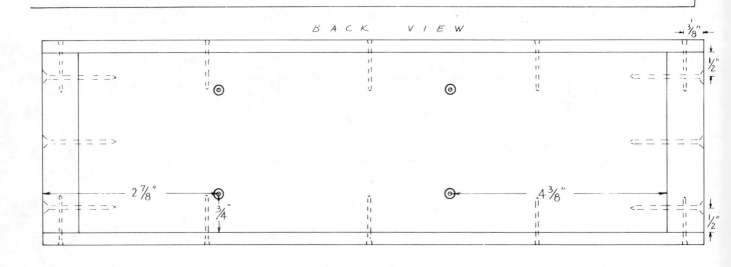

3/8"

1/2"

2 7/8"   4 3/8"

3/4"

1/2"

2
At the Firehouse

Firehouse
Pumper
Ladder Truck
Ambulance

The pumper and ladder truck are designed to be housed in the firehouse along with the ambulance. This set is likely to be especially popular with children who imagine themselves racing to the scene of a blazing fire whenever a fire truck goes by with sirens wailing. Many an imaginary fire can be put out and many a rescue accomplished with these three toys.

FIRE HOUSE

Materials

    2 pieces 3/4″ × 5 1/2″ × 12″——sides
    1 piece 3/4″ × 5 1/2″ × 14″——back
    2 pieces 1/4″ × 12 7/8″ × 15 1/2″——roof and floor—
       plywood
    2 pieces 7/16″ × 3/4″ × 5 1/2″——posts
    6   1 1/2″ no. 6 flathead screws
    No. 16   1″ brads

Construction

1. In each of the side pieces, drill and countersink three holes for the screws. Locate the holes 3/8″ from one end (rear), 3/4″ from the upper and lower edges with one in the middle (see diagram).

2. Screw the sides to the ends of the back.

3. Glue the posts to the front end of the sides.

4. In the roof and floor drill pilot holes for the brads 3/8″ from the side and back edges. The holes along the sides are 3/4″ from the back edge and spaced 2 3/4″ apart. The three holes along the back are in 4″ from either end with one midway between the other two.

5. Before nailing the floor on, saw along one edge (front) with the saw tilted at 40 degrees.

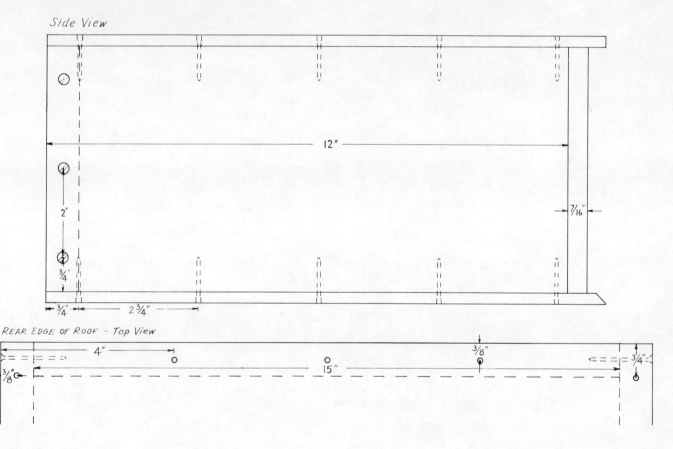

Side View

REAR EDGE OF ROOF - Top View

33

PUMPER

Materials

    1 piece 7/16″ × 1 1/2″ × 6 1/2″——frame
    1 piece 1 1/8″ × 2″ × 2″——A } cab and engine
    1 piece 3/4″ × 2″ × 2″——B
    1 piece 1 1/8″ × 1″ × 3/4″——C
    2 pieces 3/4″ × 1″ × 1 1/4″ } D—pump panel section
    1 piece 7/16″ × 1″ × 1 1/4″
    2 pieces 1/4″ dowel 1/2″ long } hose connectors
    4 pieces 1/8″ dowel 1/2″ long
    2 pieces 1/8″ × 1/2″ × 1 3/4″——sides
    2 pieces 1/4″ × 1/2″ × 5/8″——ends } hose rack
    2 pieces 1/2″ dowel 5/8″ long——reels
    1 piece 3/4″ × 1 3/4″ × 2 1/2″
    1 piece 7/16″ × 1 3/4″ × 2 1/2″ } tank
    2 pieces 1/8″ × 1 3/4″ × 2 1/2″——sides

34

2 pieces 5/8″ × 3/4″ × 1 1/2″——axle holders
1 piece 1/4″ × 1/2″ × 2 1/8″——bumper—hardwood
4 pieces 1/8″ × 3/16″ × 2 1/2″——rails—
   plywood   } ladder
18 pieces applicator sticks——1/2″ long—rungs ⌡
2 small furniture nails——headlights
1 piece 3/8″ dowel 1/2″ long (or use axle pin)——
   light on cab
1 piece 3/16″ dowel 2 1/8″ long——front axle
1 piece 3/16″ dowel 2 5/8″ long——rear axle
6   1″ wheels

Construction

1. With the saw tilted at 15 degrees saw off the front and rear edges of the B piece. Glue B to A.

2. Drive in the headlights 3/4″ from the lower edge and 1/4″ from the side edges.

3. In the top of the cab drill a 3/8″ hole about 1/4″ deep, 1/2″ from the front edge and centered for the warning light.

4. Make the axle holders (see page 7). Lengthwise through the center of each drill a 7/32″ hole. Glue the front holder to the frame 1/2″ from the end and the rear holder 1″ from the end.

5. Glue the cab to the frame letting it extend 3/16″ beyond the end.

6. Round off the ends of the bumper and glue it to the frame.

7. Center the C piece on the frame and glue it to the frame and cab. An 1 1/8″ × 1″ side should be against the cab.

8. Glue the three D pieces together with the 7/16″ piece in the middle. In each 1″ × 1 1/4″ side drill holes for the hose connectors (see diagram).

9. Glue the D piece, or pump panel section, to the frame and against the C piece.

10. Make the hose rack by gluing one side to the ends. Glue the reels to the side. Attach the other side and glue the assembly to the top of D.

11. Glue the two pieces together to make the tank. Round off the upper corners of the sides and glue them to the tank. Glue the tank to the frame and against the pump section.

12. To make the ladder rails, draw parallel lines 1/4″ apart on a piece of 1/8″ plywood. Use the try square as a guide. Draw the first line 3/8″ from one end which will be the lower end of the ladder. Saw off four strips 3/16″ wide. In the center of each line drill a hole about 3/32″ deep. A no. 44 drill is just right for this.

13. Put glue on one end of the rungs and insert them into one rail. Apply glue again and fit the rungs into the other rail.

14. Glue the ladders to the sides of the tank about 3/8″ down from the top edge with the foot of the ladder to the rear.

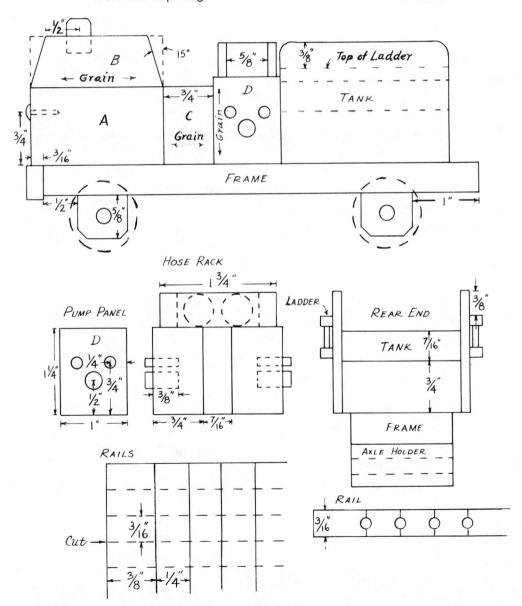

LADDER TRUCK

Materials

1 piece 7/16″ × 1 1/2″ × 8″——frame
1 piece 1 1/8″ × 2″ × 2″——A } cab
1 piece 3/4″ × 2″ × 2″——B
1 piece 3/4″ × 2″ × 5 3/4″——C } ladder support
3 pieces 7/16″ × 1/2″ × 2″——D
7 pieces 3/16″ dowel 3/4″ long——stakes
2 pieces 5/8″ × 3/4″ × 1 1/2″——axle holders
1 piece 1/4″ × 1/2″ × 2 1/8″——bumper——hardwood
1 piece 3/16″ dowel 2 1/8″ long——front axle
1 piece 3/16″ dowel 2 5/8″ long——rear axle
1 piece 3/8″ dowel 1/2″ long (or use axle pin)——light
    on cab
2 pieces 1/4″ × 3/8″ × 7 3/4″——rails } ladder
15 pieces 1/8″ dowel 1″ long——rungs
2 small furniture nails——headlights
6   1″ wheels

Construction

1. Saw each end of the B piece with the saw blade tilted at 15 degrees. Glue B to A to make the cab.

2. Drive in the headlights 1/4″ from the side edges and 3/4″ from the lower surface.

3. In the top of the cab drill a hole 1/2″ from the front edge and centered for the light.

4. Make the axle holders (see page 7), and drill a 7/32″ hole lengthwise through the center.

5. Glue the front axle holder to the frame 1/2″ from the end and the rear holder 1 1/2″ from the end.

6. Glue the cab to the frame letting it extend 3/16″ beyond the end.

7. Round off the ends of the bumper and glue it to the frame.

8. Glue D pieces to the upper side and even with the ends of the C piece. Glue the third D piece midway between the end pieces.

9. Then, 1/4″ from the ends of the D pieces, drill a 3/16″ hole about 1/4″ deep. In one D piece, which will be the rear one, drill a similar hole midway between the end holes.

10. Insert the stakes into the holes.

11. Glue the ladder support to the frame and against the cab.

12. To make the ladder rails, draw parallel lines 1/2″ apart on a piece of 1/4″ stock 7/8″ or so wide. Use the try square as a guide. Locate the first line 1/2″ from one end, which will be the lower end of the ladder. Saw two strips 3/8″ wide from the piece for the rails.

13. In the center of each line drill a hole about 1/8″ in depth. A no. 29 drill is just right for an 1/8″ rung.

14. Put a little glue on one end of each rung and insert it into one rail.

15. Again apply glue and fit the rungs into the other rail.

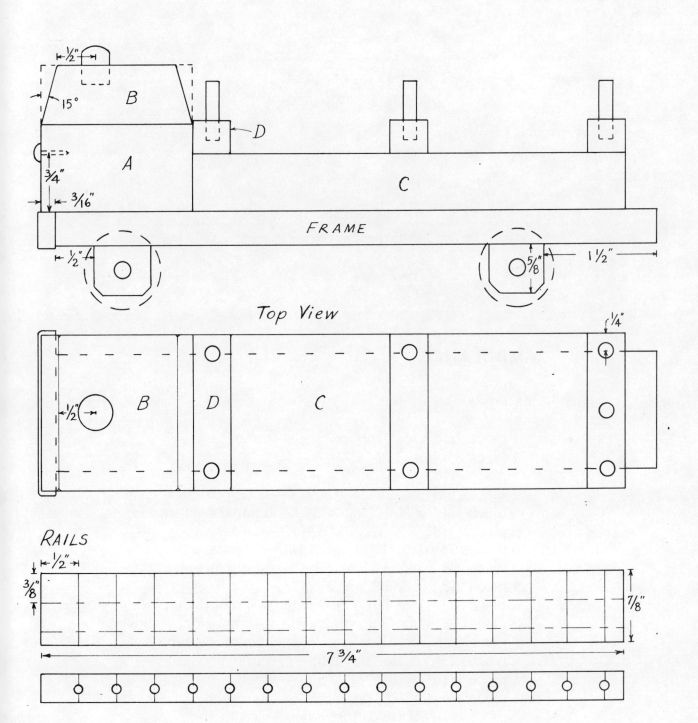

½"

15°

B

A

¾"

³⁄₁₆"

D

C

FRAME

½"

⅝"

1½"

Top View

¼"

½"

B

D

C

RAILS

½"

⅜"

⅞"

7¾"

AMBULANCE

Materials

```
1 piece 7/16" × 1 1/2" × 5"——frame
1 piece 3/4" × 2" × 2"——A   ⎫
                             ⎬ cab and hood
1 piece 7/16" × 2" × 1"——B  ⎭
2 pieces 5/8" × 3/4" × 1 1/2"——axle holders
1 piece 1/4" × 1/2" × 2 1/8"——bumper—hardwood
2 pieces 1/8" × 1 1/2" × 3 1/4"——sides
2 pieces 7/16" × 1 1/2" × 2 1/8"——ends
1 piece 1/8" × 2 3/8" × 3 1/4"——bottom—plywood
1 piece 1/8" × 2 3/8" × 3 1/4"——roof
1 piece 1/8" × 2 1/16" × 2 5/16"——roof underpiece
2 pieces 3/16" × 3/8" × 2 3/8"——light holders—box
1 piece 3/16" × 3/8" × 2"——light holder—cab
6 pieces 1/4" dowel 3/8" long——warning lights
1 piece 7/16" × 3/4" × 2 3/8"——cot
1 piece 1/4" × 1/2" × 1 1/2"——step
1 piece 3/16" dowel 2 1/8" long——front axle
1 piece 3/16" dowel 2 5/8" long——rear axle
2 small furniture nails——headlights
6      1" wheels
```

40

Construction

1. Round off one edge (front) of the A piece and sand the upper surface. Saw one end of the B piece with the saw set at 15 degrees. Glue B to A and round off the back edge of B.

2. Drive in the headlights about 1/2″ from the lower surface and 1/4″ from the side edges.

3. Shape the axle holders as in the diagram. Drill a 7/32″ hole lengthwise through the center of each (see page 7).

4. Glue the front axle holder to the frame 1/4″ from the end and the rear holder 3/4″ from the end.

5. Glue the cab assembly to the frame letting it extend 3/16″ beyond the end of the frame.

6. Round off the ends of the bumper and glue it to the frame.

7. In one end piece (back) cut an opening 1 1/8″ wide and 1 1/4″ high for the doorway.

8. Glue the sides to the ends and attach the bottom. Glue the box to the frame and against the cab.

9. Center the underpiece on the roof and glue in place.

10. In each light holder drill a 1/4″ hole 3/8″ from the ends.

11. Round off one end of the warning lights and insert them into the holes.

12. Glue the shorter holder to the cab roof.

13. Glue the other holders to the box roof 1/4″ from the ends.

14. Glue the step to the end of the frame.

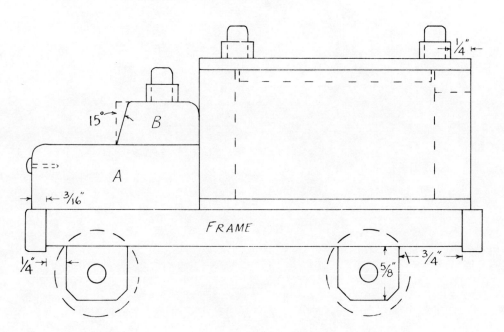

41

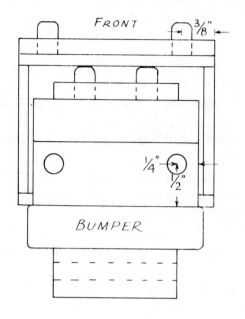

FRONT

BUMPER

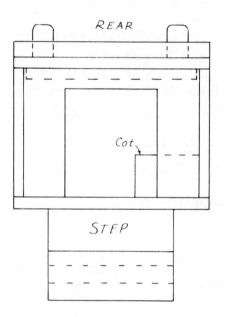

REAR

Cot

STEP

42

3
On the Farm

Barn

Garden Tractor and Cart

Pickup Truck

Tractor and Trailer

Hay Wagon

Every farmer needs a large tractor to pull the various pieces of farm equipment. He also finds a small tractor handy to use in the garden or around the lawn. And naturally he'd find it difficult to get along well without a pickup truck to haul produce to market or to pick up supplies in town. Of course there are numerous other pieces of farm equipment, and you may find that you will want to design others that can be attached to the tractors. A visit to a farm or a farm equipment outlet can provide you with many ideas for more pieces.

BARN

Materials

2 pieces 3/4″ × 8 1/2″ × 9″——ends
1 piece 3/4″ × 8 1/2″ × 14″——floor
2 pieces 1/4″ × 5 1/2″ × 16″——roof—plywood
2 pieces 1/4″ × 4 3/4″ × 6 1/4″ } siding for front
1 piece 1/4″ × 6″ × 1″
2 pieces 3/4″ × 1 1/4″ × 14″——ridge brace
2 pieces 3/4″ × 1″ × 14″——braces—front and back
1 piece 3/4″ × 6″ × 3″——ramp
6   2″ no. 6 flathead screws
8   1 1/2″ no. 6 flathead screws
No. 16   1″ brads
No. 16   3/4″ brads

44

Construction

1. Across one edge (upper) of one end piece draw a line midway or 4 1/4″ from the side edges. Set the miter gauge at 60 degrees. With the end of the piece against the wood facing, fastened to the miter gauge, saw from this line to the edge thus removing the corner. Turn the piece over and repeat the operation. If a stop is fastened, with a C clamp, to the facing and against the back edge of the piece, it will prevent creeping.

2. In each end, drill and countersink seven holes for screws as shown in the diagram.

3. Screw the ends to the floor, using the 2″ screws.

4. Set the saw at 30 degrees and saw off one 3/4″ side of each ridge brace piece. When the 1 1/4″ sides are glued together, they will form the same angle as the ends. Set the brace in place and drive in the screws.

5. Install the front and back braces. They should be even with the edges of the ends.

6. With the saw tilted at 30 degrees, saw a narrow strip lengthwise off one edge of each roof piece. The underside of the pieces should face upward when making these cuts. When the two pieces are joined at the peak, they will form the angle of the ends.

7. In the siding for the front drill pilot holes for the brads 3/8″ from the edges. The holes along the top and bottom are 2″ apart. The holes at the sides are 3 1/8″ from the bottom edge.

8. Nail the siding to the floor, ends, and brace leaving a 6″ wide doorway. Glue the 1″ piece of siding to the brace above the doorway.

9. In each roof board drill pilot holes for the brads. The end holes are in 5/8″ and spaced 1 1/4″ apart starting at the lower edge. The holes along the upper edge are 4 1/2″ and 8″ from the ends and 3/8″ from the edge. Use 3/4″ brads when nailing the roof boards to the ridge brace.

10. Install one side of the roof. It will extend 1/4″ at each end. Set the other piece in place against the first so as to form a tight joint at the peak and nail it fast. Three 3/4″ brads, evenly spaced on each side, 3/8″ from the peak should be sufficient.

11. Saw off one end of the ramp with the saw set at 45 degrees. The ramp may be glued to the edge of the floor.

12. The back of the barn has been left open for easy access. It may be sided or partially sided, as was the front.

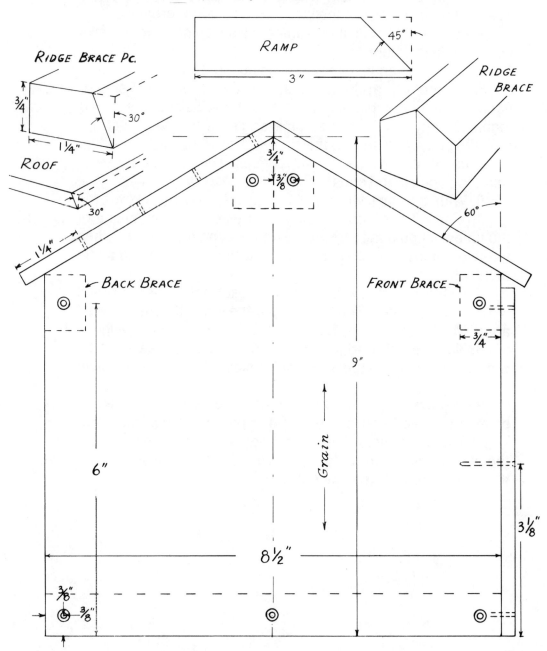

GARDEN TRACTOR AND CART

Materials: Tractor

2 pieces 7/16″ × 1″ × 5 1/4″——A ⎤
1 piece 7/16″ × 3/4″ × 5 1/4″——B ⎬ frame
1 piece 7/16″ × 1/4″ × 6 1/4″——hitch bar ⎦
1 piece 3/4″ × 1 5/16″ × 3″——engine
1 piece 1/2″ dowel 3/4″ long——seat
1 piece 3/4″ dowel 1 1/4″ long——axle holder
1 piece 1/4″ dowel 1″ long——hitch
1 piece 1/4″ dowel 2 5/8″ long——front axle
1 piece 1/4″ dowel 3 3/8″ long——rear axle
1 piece 3/16″ dowel 1″ long——steering wheel shaft
1   3/4″ wheel——steering wheel
4 beads about 1/2″ long and 1/2″ diameter (or use 1/4″
    ferrules) —— spacers
2   1 1/4″ wheels
2   2 1/2″ wheels

47

Construction

1. Glue the B piece between the A pieces so that the top edges are even. Then, 3/8" from one end of the hitch bar, drill a 1/4" hole equidistant from the side edges. Round off this end. Glue the bar in the opening in the frame. It will extend 1" at the rear. Sand the upper surface of the frame.

2. Drill a 9/32" hole through the frame 1" from the rear end and 3/8" from the lower edge.

3. In the upper surface of the frame drill a 1/2" hole 3/8" deep and 1 1/4" from the rear end for the seat. The hole should be midway between the side edges.

4. In the underside of the frame drill a 3/4" hole 5/8" deep 3/4" from the front end and centered, for the axle holder.

5. In the rear end of the engine drill a 7/32" hole 1/2" deep 1/4" down from the upper edge and centered, for the steering shaft.

6. Glue the engine to the frame even with the front end.

7. Drill a 9/32" hole through the axle holder 3/8" from one end. Glue the holder in the hole in the frame.

8. Glue the steering wheel on the shaft and insert it into the hole in the engine. Install the seat.

9. Insert the hitch into the hole in the bar. It should extend upward.

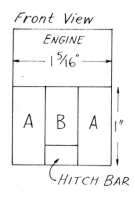

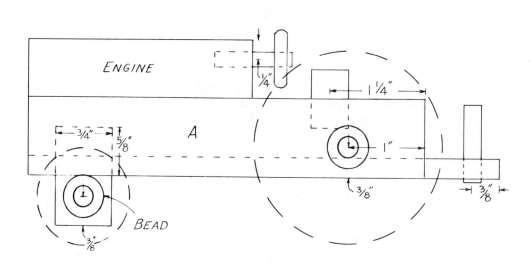

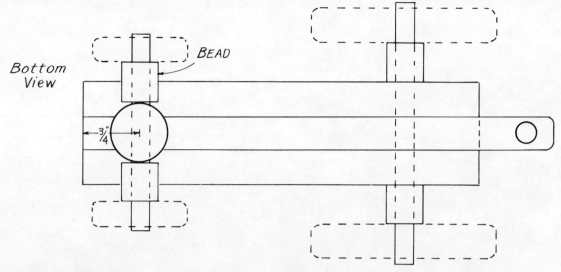

Bottom View

BEAD

3/4"

Materials: Cart

2 pieces 7/16″ × 3/4″ × 1 3/4″——ends }
2 pieces 1/4″ × 3/4″ × 3 1/4″——sides } box
1 piece 1/8″ × 2 1/4″ × 3 1/4″——bottom }
1 piece 3/4″ × 1″ × 2 1/4″——axle holder
1 piece 1/4″ × 1/2″ × 2 1/4″——tongue
1 piece 1/4″ dowel 3 1/4″ long——axle
2   1 1/4″ wheels

Construction

1. Assemble the box by gluing the sides to the ends and putting on the bottom.

2. Shape the axle holder (see page 7). Drill a 9/32″ hole lengthwise through the holder 3/8″ from the lower edge.

3. Glue the axle holder to the box 1 5/16″ from one end (front).

4. Drill a 9/32″ hole 3/8″ from one end of the tongue. Round off this end.

5. Center the tongue on the box against the axle holder and glue in place.

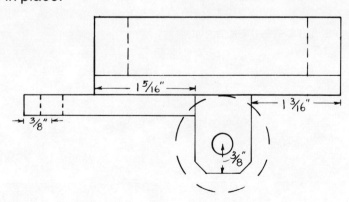

1 5/16″   1 3/16″

3/8″   3/8″

PICKUP TRUCK

Materials

1 piece 7/16″ × 1 3/4″ × 6 3/4″——frame
1 piece 1 1/8″ × 2 1/2″ × 3 1/4″——A ⎫
1 piece 3/4″ × 2 1/2″ × 1 1/2″——B ⎬ cab and hood
2 pieces 7/16″ × 1″ × 2″——ends ⎫
2 pieces 1/4″ × 1″ × 4″——sides ⎬ box
1 piece 1/4″ × 2 1/2″ × 4″——bottom ⎭
1 piece 1/4″ × 1/2″ × 2 3/4″——bumper—hardwood
2 pieces 3/4″ × 1″ × 1 3/4″——axle holders
1 piece 1/4″ dowel 2 5/8″ long——front axle
1 piece 1/4″ dowel 3 3/8″ long——rear axle
2 furniture nails——headlights
6   1 1/4″ wheels

Construction

1. Shape the axle holders (see page 7). Drill a 9/32″ hole lengthwise through the center of each.
2. Glue the front holder to the frame 1/4″ from the end and the rear holder 1/2″ from the end.
3. Round off one top edge (front) of the A piece and sand the upper surface. Set the saw at 15 degrees and saw off one end of the B piece. Glue B to A and round off the back edge of B.
4. Drive in the headlights 1/4″ from the side edges and 3/4″ from the lower edge.
5. Glue the sides of the box to the ends and attach the bottom.
6. Glue the cab assembly to the frame letting it extend 3/16″ beyond the end.
7. Glue the bumper to the end of the frame.
8. Glue the box to the frame and against the cab.

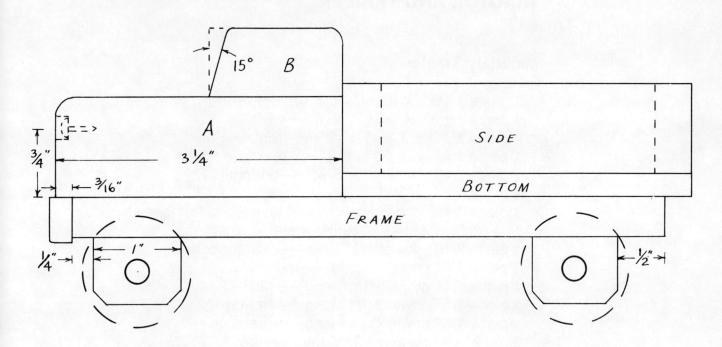

TRACTOR AND TRAILER

Materials: Tractor

1 piece 1 1/8″ × 1 1/4″ × 6 1/2″——A
1 piece 1 1/8″ × 1 1/4″ × 4″——B
1 piece 3/4″ × 1 3/4″ × 2″——front axle holder
1 piece 3/4″ × 1 1/4″ × 3″——rear axle holder
1 piece 7/16″ × 3/4″ × 5/8″——bottom ⎫
1 piece 1/4″ × 3/4″ × 1″——back ⎬ seat
1 piece 3/16″ dowel about 1 1/2″ long——steering shaft
1   3/4″ wheel——steering wheel
1 piece 3/16″ dowel 1/2″ long——radiator cap
1 piece 1/4″ dowel 1″ long——muffler
1 piece 1/4″ dowel 1 1/4″ long——hitch
1 piece 1/4″ dowel 3 1/4″ long——front axle
1 piece 1/4″ dowel 4 3/4″ long——rear axle
2   2″ wheels about 1/2″ thick——front
2   3″ wheels about 3/4″ thick——rear

Construction

1. Saw grooves, across the grain, in the bottom of the A piece 1/2" deep and 3/4" wide. Locate the front groove 5/8" from the end and the rear groove 1 1/4" from the end. Drill a 1/4" hole 1/2" deep for the hitch 1/2" from the end and centered.

2. Lengthwise through each axle holder drill a 9/32" hole 3/8" from one edge (lower) and centered.

3. Drill a hole slightly larger than 3/16" in one end (rear) of the B piece 1/4" from the upper edge, 1" deep, and centered for the steering shaft.

4. In the B piece drill a 3/16" hole for the radiator cap 3/8" from the end and about 3/8" deep. Also drill a 1/4" hole for the muffler 1/2" in from one side edge, 1/2" deep, and 1 1/2" from the back end.

5. Sand the upper surface of A and glue B to it so the two pieces are even at the front end.

6. Glue the axle holders in the grooves made for them.

7. Drive in the muffler and the radiator cap.

8. Install the steering wheel. Make the seat and glue in place behind the wheel. When the steering wheel is pulled out, it should hit the back of the seat thus making it nonremovable.

9. Drive the hitch into the hole. It should extend about 3/4".

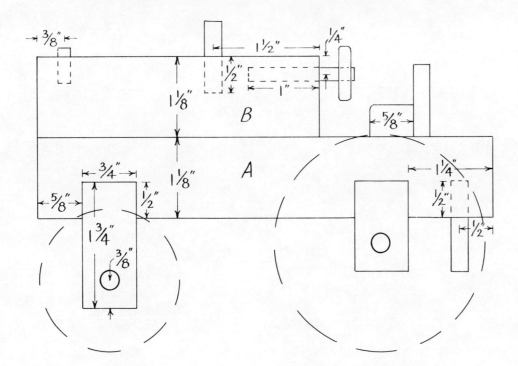

Materials: Trailer

2 pieces 7/16″ × 1 1/4″ × 6″ ⎫
1 piece 7/16″ × 3/4″ × 8 1/2″ ⎬ deck
2 pieces 3/4″ × 1 1/8″ × 2 1/4″——axle holders
1 piece 7/16″ × 3/4″ × 3 3/4″——brace
2 pieces 1/4″ dowel 3 1/4″ long——axles
4   1 1/4″ wheels

Construction

1. Drill a 9/32″ hole 3/8″ from one end of the 8 1/2″ piece equidistant from the edges.

2. Glue the three deck pieces together, with the longer one in the middle.

3. Shape the axle holders (see page 7). Drill a 9/32″ hole lengthwise through each one, 3/8″ from the lower edge and centered.

4. Glue the brace to the underside of the deck equidistant from the ends and side edges.

5. Glue the axle holders to the deck against the ends of the brace and 1/2″ in from the side edges.

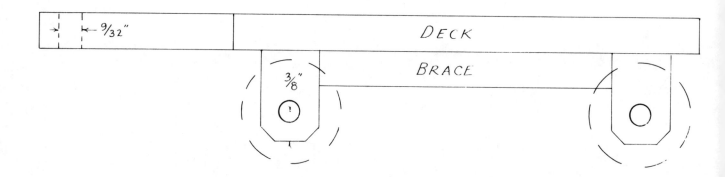

HAY WAGON

Materials

1 piece 7/16″ × 3″ × 6″——deck
2 pieces 7/16″ × 2 1/2″ × 3″——ends
2 pieces 1/4″ × 1/2″ × 6 1/2″——frame
1 piece 1/4″ × 1/2″ × 9″——tongue
2 pieces 3/4″ × 1″ × 2 1/4″——axle holders
2 pieces 1/4″ dowel 3 1/8″ long——axles
4   1 1/4″ wheels

Construction

1. Round off two corners (upper) of the ends and glue them to the ends of the deck.

2. Shape the axle holders (see page 7). Drill a 9/32″ hole lengthwise through them, 3/8″ from the lower surface and centered.

3. Glue the frame pieces to the axle holders 1/8″ from the ends of the holders. The frame pieces should extend 3/4″ beyond the holders.

4. Drill a 9/32″ hole 1/2″ from one end of the tongue and equidistant from the side edges.

5. Glue the tongue to the axle holders equidistant from the frame pieces and even with the back ends.

6. To strengthen the frame, 3/16″ dowel pegs 1/2″ long may be driven into holes made in the frame pieces, tongue, and axle holders. The end pieces may also be doweled to the deck.

7. Center the deck on the frame and glue it fast.

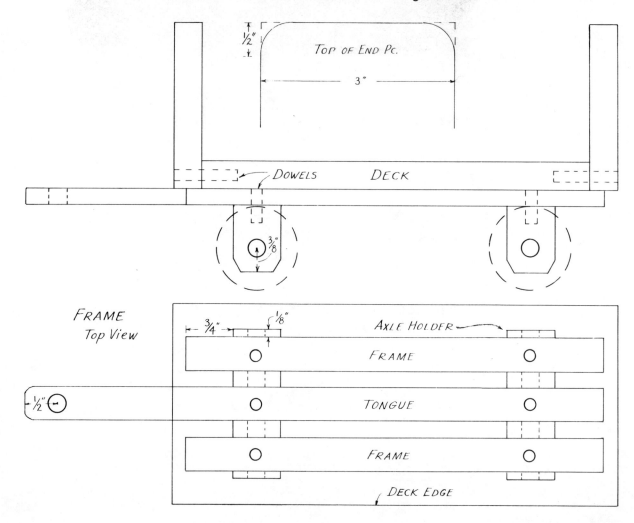

4
On the Highway

Gasoline Service Island
Automobile and Boat Trailer
Travel Trailer
Cabover Tractor and Flatbed Hauler
Cabover with Sleeper Tractor and Semi-Trailer
Extended Nose with Sleeper Tractor
   and Open-Top Trailer

Here are the eighteen-wheelers most commonly seen on local and interstate highways. The four different tractors may be used with any of the trailers. You may want to incorporate the service station described in chapter 1 into this set. To make them large enough and sturdy enough for a child to play with, the automobiles with their trailers come out fairly large in comparison with the trucks. Suggestions for making a larger open-top trailer and tractor are given in the introduction, and you can adapt these suggestions to other toys here and throughout the book if you prefer a somewhat larger toy.

GASOLINE SERVICE ISLAND

Materials

    1 piece 7/16″ × 2 1/2″ × 8″——platform
    1 piece 1/4″ × 2 3/4″ × 8″——roof
    2 pieces 1/4″ × 1/2″ × 2 3/4″——roof supports
    2 pieces 1/4″ dowel 4 1/2″ long——posts
    2 pieces 3/4″ × 1 1/8″ × 2 1/8″——pumps
    1 round black shoelace——hose

Construction

1. Glue the supports to the underside of the roof 2 1/4″ from the ends.

2. In the center of each support drill a 1/4″ hole about 3/8″ deep.

3. In the platform drill two 1/4″ holes about 5/16″ in depth 2 1/2″ from either end and centered.

4. Drill two holes in one 3/4″ side of each pump. The size of the holes will depend on the size of the shoelace used. The holes can be located side by side or one above the other. In the latter case, the hole for the hose should be the lower one and a smaller hole for the metal end should be the upper one.

5. Cut off a four- or five-inch piece from each end of the lace. Put some glue in the hole and insert the end of the lace.

6. Glue the pumps to the platform 1/2″ from the ends and equidistant from the side edges.

7. Drive the posts into the holes in the platform.

8. Put glue in the holes in the supports and set the roof on the posts.

ROOF – Underside

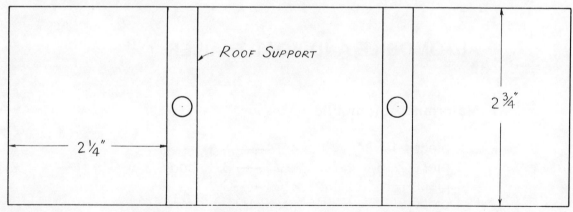

PUMP

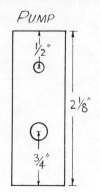

59

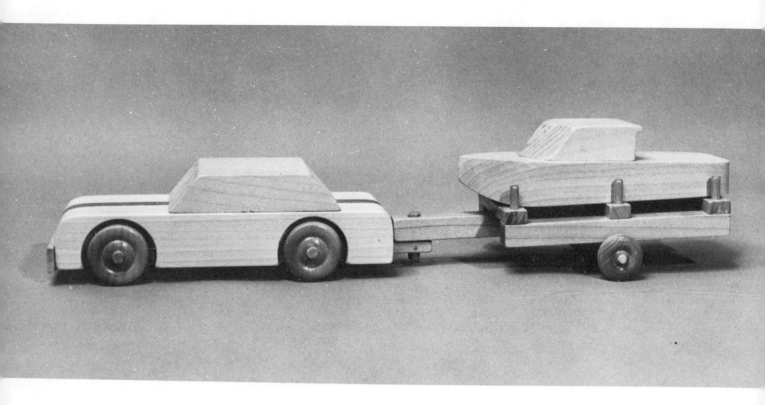

AUTOMOBILE AND BOAT TRAILER

Materials: Automobile

2 pieces 1 1/8″ × 1″ × 7″——A ⎫
1 piece 7/16″ × 7/8″ × 7″——B ⎬ body
1 piece 7/16″ × 1/4″ × 8″——C ⎭
1 piece 3/4″ × 2 5/16″ × 3 1/2″——roof
1 piece 3/16″ × 3/8″ × 2 5/8″——bumper—hardwood
2 pieces 1/4″ dowel 2 3/4″ long——axles
2 furniture nails——headlights
1 piece 1/4″ dowel 1″ long——hitch
4   1 1/4″ wheels

60

Construction

1. Glue the B piece between the A pieces even with one surface (upper) of the A pieces.

2. Round off the upper edges of the ends and sand.

3. Drive in the headlights about 5/8" from the lower surface and 1/4" from the side edges.

4. Drill a 1/4" hole 3/8" from one end and centered in the C piece. Glue the piece in the opening in the bottom. It will extend 1" at the rear.

5. With a 1 1/2" Greenlee type bit, drill the wheel wells to a depth of 3/8" or the thickness of the wheels being used. Locate the front well 1 1/4" from the end and the rear well 1 3/4" from the end. The center of each well should be up 1/4" from the lower edge.

6. Through the center of each well drill a 9/32" hole.

7. Drive the dowel hitch into the hole in the C piece. It should extend upward.

8. Saw each end of the roof at a 40-degree angle and along the side edges with the saw set at 5 degrees.

9. Glue the roof to the body about 2 1/2" from the front end.

10. Install the bumper.

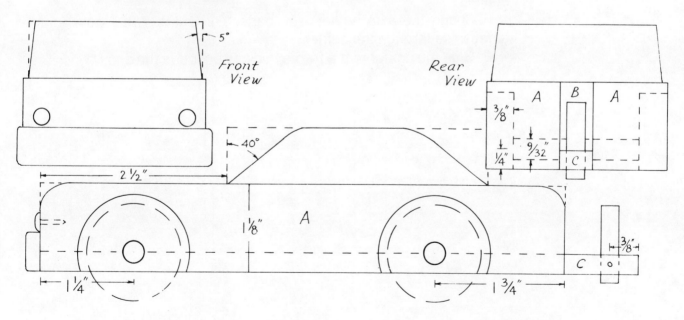

Materials: Trailer

2 pieces 7/16″ × 1/2″ × 5″——A } frame
3 pieces 1/4″ × 1/2″ × 2 3/4″——B }
1 piece 7/16″ × 1/2″ × 7″——tongue
1 piece 5/8″ × 3/4″ × 2 3/4″——axle holder
1 piece 3/16″ dowel 3 3/8″ long——axle
6 pieces 3/16″ dowel 1″ long——stakes
2   1″ wheels

Construction

1. Glue the B pieces to the A pieces, even with the ends and side edges of A. A piece of scrap material 1 3/4″ wide and four or five inches long placed between the A pieces will make it easier to glue the parts together.

2. Glue the third B piece midway between the end pieces.

3. Drill a 9/32″ hole 3/8″ from one end of the tongue and centered.

4. Then 3/16″ from the ends of each B piece drill a 3/16″ hole about 1/2″ deep and centered for the stakes. Drive in the stakes.

5. Shape the axle holder (see page 7). Drill a 7/32″ hole lengthwise through the center.

6. Glue the holder to the frame midway between the ends.

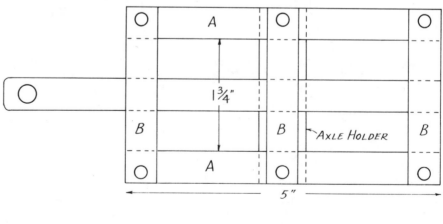

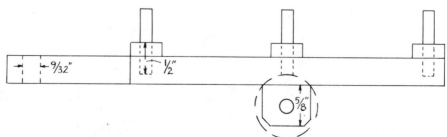

TRAVEL TRAILER

Materials

2 pieces 1/4″ × 2″ × 6 3/4″ } sides
2 pieces 1/4″ × 1/2″ × 6 3/4″ }
1 piece 7/16″ × 2 1/2″ × 2 1/8″——front end
1 piece 7/16″ × 2″ × 2 1/8″ } rear end
1 piece 7/16″ × 1/2″ × 2 1/8″ }
1 piece 1/4″ × 2 5/8″ × 6 3/4″——bottom
1 piece 1/4″ × 2 5/8″ × 6 3/4″ } roof
2 pieces 1/4″ × 3/4″ × 2 1/16″——A }
2 pieces 3/4″ × 7/8″ × 2″——x } axle holder
1 piece 7/16″ × 1/2″ × 2″——y }
1 piece 1/4″ × 1/2″ × 5 1/2″——hitch bar
2 pieces 3/16″ dowel 2 5/8″ long——axles
4   1″ wheels

Construction

1. In each side cut openings for windows 3/4″ × 1 1/2″. In the back end, cut an opening 1/2″ × 1 1/8″. One way to do this is to draw the side windows on a piece of stock 3/4″ × 2″ × 6 3/4″. With the saw blade 3/4″ above the table make several passes through the piece. Then rip out the 1/4″ sides. Use the same procedure for the rear window except for the ripping.

2. Across one side section make two shallow, narrow saw cuts 3/4″ apart and 3″ from either end to represent a door.

3. Glue the 1/2″ pieces to the sides and rear end piece and sand.

4. Glue the sides to the ends, the side with the door being the right side.

5. Glue on the bottom.

6. Glue the two A pieces to the underside of the roof 1/2″ from the ends and equidistant from the side edges.

7. Make the axle holder (see page 7). Drill 7/32″ holes lengthwise through each x piece 1/4″ from the lower edge.

8. Saw a groove across the grain in the axle holder 1/2″ wide and 1/4″ deep for the hitch bar.

9. Drill a 9/32″ hole 3/8″ from one end of the bar and centered.

10. Glue the bar in the groove so it is even with the back edge of the axle holder.

11. Glue the axle holder assembly to the bottom, midway between the ends.

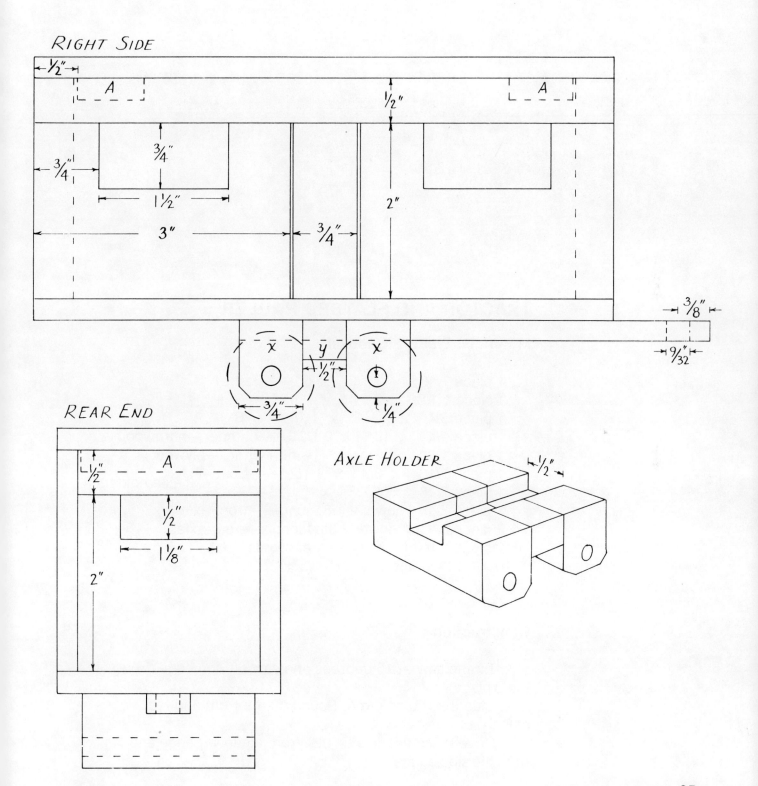

RIGHT SIDE

REAR END

AXLE HOLDER

65

TRACTOR AND FLATBED HAULER

Materials: Tractor (Cabover)

```
1 piece 7/16″ × 1 1/2″ × 5″——frame
1 piece 1 1/8″ × 2 1/4″ × 1 1/2″——A ⎫
1 piece 3/4″ × 2 1/4″ × 1 1/2″——B ⎭ cab and engine
1 piece 1/4″ × 1/2″ × 2 1/2″——bumper—hardwood
1 piece 1/8″ × 1″ × 1″——fifth wheel—plywood
1 piece 7/16″ × 3/4″ × 1 1/2″——front ⎫
1 piece 7/16″ × 1 7/8″ × 1 1/2″——rear ⎭ axle holders
1 piece 3/16″ dowel 2 1/8″ long——front axle
2 pieces 3/16″ dowel 2 5/8″ long——rear axles
2 small furniture nails——headlights
10      1″ wheels
```

Construction

1. Tilt the saw at 15 degrees and saw off one edge (front) of the B piece.

2. Glue the B piece to A. Round off the front and rear edges of B.

3. Drive in the headlights 1/2″ from the lower edge and 1/4″ from the side edges.

4. Lengthwise through the center of the front axle holder drill a 7/32″ hole. In the rear holder drill similar holes 3/8″ from the side edges. A groove about 1/4″ × 1/4″ may be cut in the rear holder (see page 7).

5. Glue the holders to the frame 1/4″ from the ends.

6. Glue the cab assembly to the frame letting it extend 3/16″ beyond the end.

7. Round off the ends of the bumper and glue it to the frame.

8. Shape the fifth wheel. Glue it to the frame 3/4″ from the end and midway between the sides.

9. Drill a 13/32″ hole through the center of the fifth wheel about 1/2″ deep.

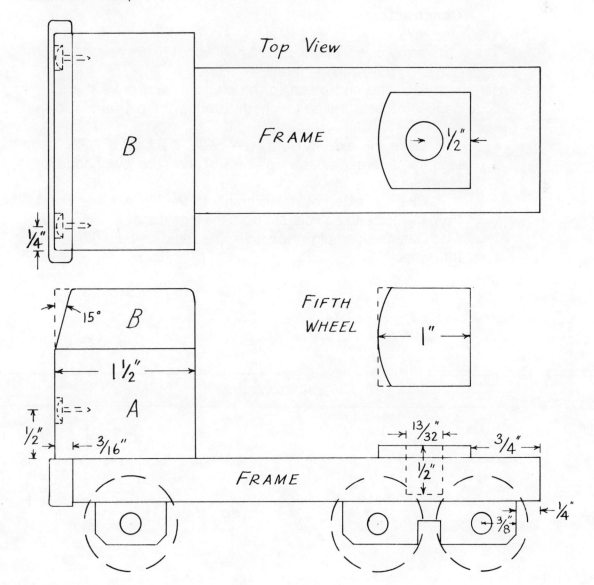

Materials: Flatbed Hauler

1 piece 7/16″ × 2 1/4″ × 9″——platform
1 piece 7/16″ × 1″ × 2 1/4″——front end
2 pieces 3/4″ × 1 3/16″ × 1 1/2″——x }
1 piece 7/16″ × 3/4″ × 1 1/2″——y } axle holder
1 piece 3/8″ dowel about 3/4″ long——king pin
2 pieces 3/16″ dowel 2 5/8″ long——axles
2 pieces 3/16″ dowel about 1″ long —— pegs
8   1″ wheels

Construction

1. In the platform drill a 3/8″ hole about 5/16″ deep, 1″ from one end (front) and centered.

2. Glue the end piece to the platform and drive the 3/16″ pegs into holes drilled for them through the platform into the end.

3. Make the axle holders (see page 7). Drill a 7/32″ hole lengthwise through each x piece 3/8″ from the lower edge and centered.

4. Glue the axle holder assembly to the bottom, about 1/4″ from the end and equidistant from the side edges.

5. Glue the king pin in the hole. The trailer should ride on the fifth wheel.

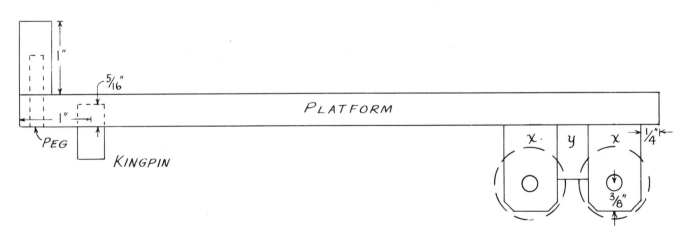

TRACTOR AND SEMI-TRAILER

Materials: Tractor (cabover with sleeper)

1 piece 7/16″ × 1 1/2″ × 5″——frame
1 piece 1 1/8″ × 2 1/4″ × 2″——A } cab and engine
1 piece 3/4″ × 2 1/4″ × 2″——B
1 piece 1/4″ × 1/2″ × 2 1/2″——bumper—hardwood
1 piece 1/8″ × 1″ × 1″——fifth wheel—plywood
1 piece 7/16″ × 3/4″ × 1 1/2″——front } axle holders
1 piece 7/16″ × 1 7/8″ × 1 1/2″——rear
1 piece 3/16″ dowel 2 1/8″ long——front axle
2 pieces 3/16″ dowel 2 5/8″ long——rear axles
2 small furniture nails——headlights
10   1″ wheels

Construction

1. Set the saw at 15 degrees and saw off one edge (front) of the B piece.

2. Glue B to A. Round off the front and rear edges of B.

3. Make a narrow saw cut in each side of the cab 5/8″ from the rear end to indicate the sleeper compartment.

4. Drive in the headlights 1/2″ from the lower edge and 1/4″ from the side edges.

5. Lengthwise through the center of the front axle holder drill a 7/32″ hole. In the rear holder drill similar holes 3/8″ from the side edges. A 1/4″ × 1/4″ groove may be cut in the rear holder (see page 7).

6. Glue the holders to the frame 1/4″ from the ends.

7. Glue the cab assembly to the frame letting it extend 3/16″ beyond the end.

8. Round off the ends of the bumper and glue it to the frame.

9. Shape the fifth wheel (see diagram). Glue it to the frame 3/4″ from the end and centered.

10. Drill a 13/32″ hole through the center of the fifth wheel to a depth of about 1/2″.

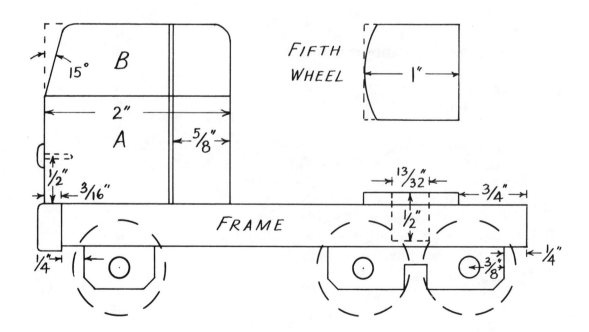

Materials: Semi-Trailer

1 piece 7/16″ × 2 1/4″ × 9″——bottom
2 pieces 7/16″ × 1 3/4″ × 1 3/4″——ends
2 pieces 1/4″ × 1 3/4″ × 9″——sides
1 piece 1/4″ × 2 1/4″ × 9″ } roof
2 pieces 1/4″ × 3/4″ × 1 11/16″——A }
2 pieces 3/4″ × 1 13/16″ × 1 1/2″——x } axle holder
1 piece 7/16″ × 3/4″ × 1 1/2″——y }
1 piece 3/8″ dowel 3/4″ long——king pin
2 pieces 3/16″ dowel 2 5/8″ long——axles
8   1″ wheels

Construction

1. Drill a 3/8″ hole about 5/16″ deep, 1″ from one end of the bottom and centered. This is for the king pin.

2. Glue the sides to the ends and put on the bottom.

3. Glue the A pieces to the roof 1/2″ from either end and equidistant from the side edges.

4. Make the axle holder (see page 7). Lengthwise through each x piece, drill a 7/32″ hole 3/8″ from the lower edge and centered.

5. Glue the axle holder to the bottom 1/4″ from the end and centered.

6. Glue the king pin in the hole. The trailer should ride on the fifth wheel.

71

TRACTOR AND TANDEM TRAILERS

Materials: Tractor (extended nose)

1 piece 7/16″ × 1 1/2″ × 5″——frame
1 piece 1 1/8″ × 2 1/4″ × 2″——A ⎫
1 piece 3/4″ × 2 1/4″ × 1 1/8″——B ⎬ cab and engine
1 piece 1/4″ × 1/2″ × 2 1/2″——bumper—hardwood
1 piece 1/8″ × 1″ × 1″——fifth wheel—plywood
1 piece 7/16″ × 3/4″ × 1 1/2″——front ⎫
1 piece 7/16″ × 1 7/8″ × 1 1/2″——rear ⎬ axle holders
1 piece 3/16″ dowel 2 1/8″ long——front axle
2 pieces 3/16″ dowel 2 5/8″ long——rear axles
2 small furniture nails——headlights
10   1″ wheels

Construction

1. With the saw tilted at 15 degrees saw off one edge (front) of the B piece.

2. Round off one edge (front) of the A piece and sand the upper surface. Glue B to A.

3. Drive in the headlights 1/2" from the lower edge and 1/4" from the side edges.

4. Lengthwise through the center of the front axle holder, drill a 7/32" hole. Drill similar holes in the rear holder 3/8" from each side edge and centered.

5. Glue the axle holders to the frame 1/4" from the ends.

6. Glue the cab assembly to the frame letting it extend 3/16" beyond the end.

7. Round off the ends of the bumper and glue it to the frame.

8. Shape the fifth wheel. Glue it in place 3/4" from the end of the frame.

9. Drill a 13/32" hole about 1/2" deep through the center of the fifth wheel.

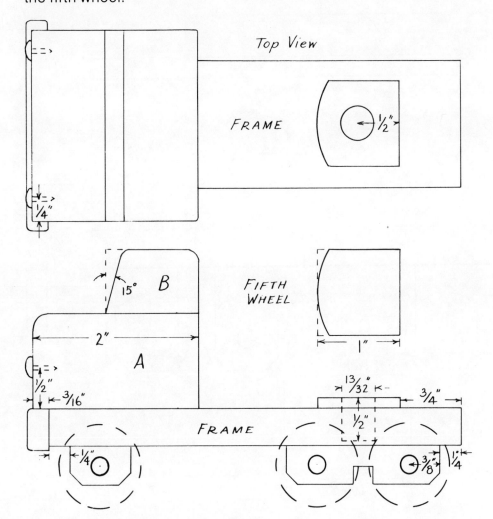

73

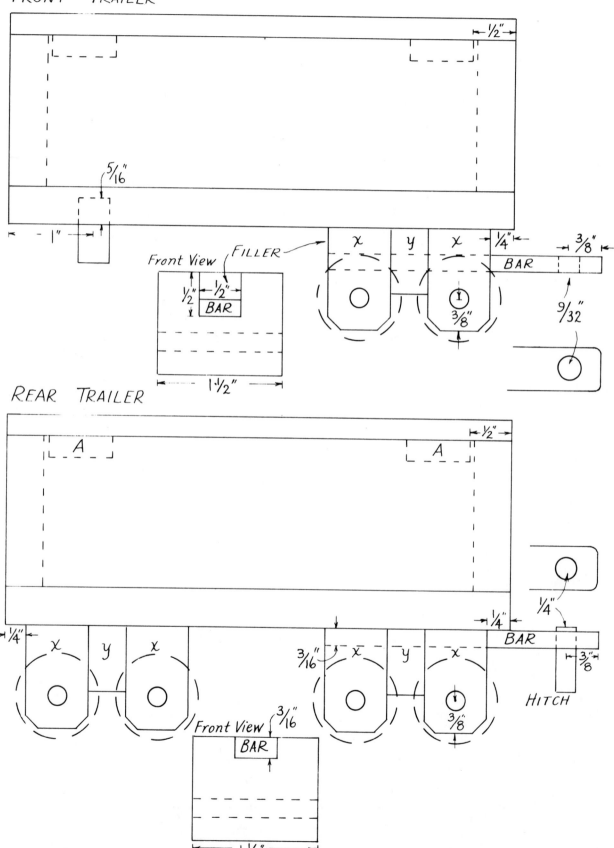

FRONT TRAILER

½"

5/16"

1"

Front View

FILLER

½" ½"

BAR

1½"

x   y   x   ¼"

BAR

3/8"

3/8"

9/32

REAR TRAILER

½"

A   A

x   y   x   ¼"

3/16"   x   y   x

BAR

¼"

¼"

BAR

3/8"

HITCH

3/8"

Front View   3/16"

BAR

3/8"

1½"

Materials: Tandem Trailers or Double Bottoms

2 pieces 7/16″ × 2 1/4″ × 6″——bottoms
4 pieces 7/16″ × 1 3/4″ × 1 3/4″——ends
4 pieces 1/4″ × 1 3/4″ × 6″——sides
2 pieces 1/4″ × 2 1/4″ × 6″ ⎫
4 pieces 1/4″ × 3/4″ × 1 11/16″——A ⎭ roofs
6 pieces 3/4″ × 1 3/16″ × 1 1/2″——x ⎫
3 pieces 7/16″ × 3/4″ × 1 1/2″——y ⎭ axle holders
1 piece 5/16″ × 1/2″ × 1 15/16″——filler
1 piece 3/8″ dowel about 3/4″ long——king pin
2 pieces 3/16″ × 1/2″ × 3 1/4″——bars ⎫
1 piece 1/4″ dowel 3/4″ long (or use axle pin)——hitch ⎭ coupling device
6 pieces 3/16″ dowel 2 5/8″ long——axles
24   1″ wheels

Construction

1. Drill a 3/8″ hole about 5/16″ deep 1″ from the end of one bottom piece and centered.

2. Glue the sides to the ends and glue on the bottoms.

3. Glue the A pieces to the roofs 1/2″ from the ends and equidistant from the side edges.

4. Make the axle holders (see page 7). Drill 7/32″ holes lengthwise through the x pieces 3/8″ from the lower edges and centered.

5. In the top surface of one axle holder assembly make a groove across the grain 1/2″ wide, 1/2″ deep, and centered for the coupler bar. Drill a 9/32″ hole in one bar 3/8″ from the end and centered. Round off the end. Glue the bar in the groove so that it extends about 1 1/4″. Glue the filler piece in the groove. It should be even with the upper surface of the axle holder. This assembly will be for the front trailer.

6. In one of the other axle holders, cut a groove 1/2″ wide and 3/16″ deep and centered.

7. Drill a 1/4″ hole 3/8″ from one end of the remaining coupler bar and round off that end. Glue the bar in the groove.

8. Glue the holders to the bottoms of the trailers 1/4″ from the ends and centered.

9. Insert the king pin into the 3/8″ hole in the front trailer and the hitch into the hole in the rear trailer coupler bar. The front trailer should ride on the fifth wheel.

TRACTOR AND OPEN-TOP TRAILER

Materials: Tractor (extended nose with sleeper)

1 piece 7/16″ × 1 1/2″ × 6″——frame
1 piece 1 1/8″ × 2 1/4″ × 2 3/4″——A } cab and engine
1 piece 3/4″ × 2 1/4″ × 1 7/8″——B }
1 piece 1/4″ × 1/2″ × 2 1/2″——bumper—hardwood
1 piece 1/8″ × 1″ × 1″——fifth wheel—plywood
1 piece 7/16″ × 3/4″ × 1 1/2″——front } axle holders
1 piece 7/16″ × 1 7/8″ × 1 1/2″——rear }
1 piece 3/16″ dowel 2 1/8″ long——front axle
2 pieces 3/16″ dowel 2 5/8″ long——rear axles
2 small furniture nails——headlights
10   1″ wheels

Construction

1. With the saw tilted at 15 degrees saw off one edge (front) of the B piece. Round off one edge (front) of the A piece and sand the upper surface. Glue B to A.

2. Make a narrow shallow saw cut in each side of the cab 3/4″ from the rear end to indicate the sleeper compartment.

3. Drive in the headlights 1/4″ from the side edges and 1/2″ from the lower edge.

4. Make the axle holders (see page 7). Lengthwise through the center of the front holder drill a 7/32″ hole. Drill similar holes in the rear axle holder 3/8″ from each side edge and centered. A 1/4″ × 1/4″ groove may be cut in the rear holder.

5. Glue the axle holders to the frame 1/4″ from the ends.

6. Glue the cab assembly to the frame letting it extend 3/16″ beyond the end.

7. Round off the ends of the bumper and glue it to the frame.

8. Shape the fifth wheel (see diagram). Glue it in place 3/4″ from the end of the frame and centered.

9. In the center of the fifth wheel drill a 13/32″ hole about 1/2″ deep for the king pin.

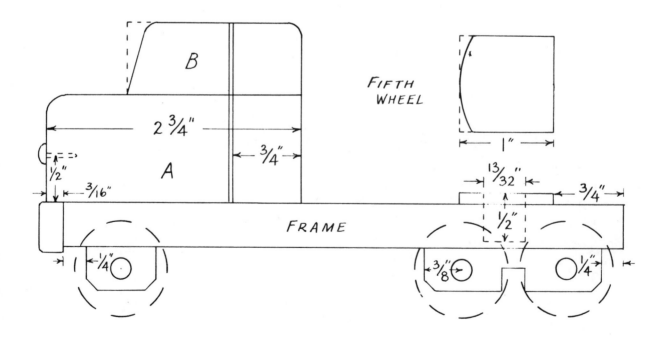

Materials: Open-Top Trailer

1 piece 7/16″ × 2 1/4″ × 9″——bottom
2 pieces 7/16″ × 1 1/2″ × 1 3/4″——ends
2 pieces 1/4″ × 1 1/2″ × 9″——sides
2 pieces 3/4″ × 1 3/16″ × 1 1/2″——x }
1 piece 7/16″ × 3/4″ × 1 1/2″——y } axle holder
1 piece 3/8″ dowel about 3/4″ long——king pin
2 pieces 3/16″ 2 5/8″ long——axles
8   1″ wheels

Construction

1. Drill a 3/8″ hole about 5/16″ deep 1″ from one end of the bottom and centered.
2. Glue the sides to the ends and glue on the bottom.
3. Make the axle holder (see page 7). Lengthwise through each x piece drill a 7/32″ hole, 3/8″ from the lower edge and centered.
4. Glue the axle holder to the bottom 1/4″ from the end and equidistant from the side edges.
5. Glue the king pin in the hole. The trailer should ride on the fifth wheel.

5
Building a Highway

Dump Truck
Rock Hauler
Dump Trailer and Tractor
Road Grader
Double Drum Roller

In this set are a heavy-duty rock hauler and dump truck used for carrying rocks and dirt to or from the construction site. The dump trailer is used to haul in fill, which is then leveled off by the grader. Then the roadbed is made smooth with the roller.

The wheels on the trucks and grader shown in the photographs have been made with a hole saw as described in the introduction ("A Word about Wheels"). Dark-colored wood was used for the wheels to contrast with the lighter wood of the frames. You can, of course, use prefabricated wheels instead.

DUMP TRUCK

Materials

3 pieces 3/4″ × 3/4″ × 7″——frame
1 piece 1 1/8″ × 2 1/4″ × 2 3/4″——A ⎱ cab and
1 piece 3/4″ × 2 1/4″ × 1 3/8″——B ⎰ engine assembly
1 piece 1/2″ × 3/4″ × 2 1/2″——bumper-hardwood
2 pieces 7/16″ × 1 1/2″ × 2 1/4″——axle holders
1 piece 7/16″ × 1 1/2″ × 2 3/4″——front end ⎤
1 piece 7/16″ × 1 1/2″ × 2 11/16″——tailgate ⎥
2 pieces 7/16″ × 1 1/2″ × 5″——sides ⎥ box
1 piece 1/4″ × 3 5/8″ × 5″——bottom—plywood ⎥
2 pieces 3/16″ dowel 1″ long——pegs——tailgate ⎥
1 piece 1/4″ dowel 3/4″ long——dumping lever ⎦
1 piece 1/4″ dowel 2 1/2″ long——peg
1 piece 1/4″ dowel 3 1/2″ long——front axle
1 piece 1/4″ dowel 4 1/2″ long——rear axle
2 small furniture nails——headlights
6   1 1/2″ wheels

82

Construction

1. Round off the upper front edge of the A piece and sand the upper surface. Saw off one end (front) of the B piece at a 15-degree angle. Glue B to A and round off the rear end of B.

2. Install the headlights about 1/4″ in from the side edges of A and 3/4″ from the lower edge.

3. In the center of each axle holder saw a groove about 9/32″ × 9/32″ (see page 7).

4. In each frame piece drill a hole slightly larger than 1/4″, 3/8″ from one end and centered. Or, in a piece of wood 3/4″ × 2 5/8″ or so, drill the hole crossways 3/8″ from one end. Then cut the piece into 3/4″ wide strips.

5. Saw off a 1 1/2″ piece from one frame piece where the hole was drilled. Save this piece.

6. Glue the three pieces together with the shorter piece in the middle. The holes should be exactly opposite each other. Round off the ends of the outside pieces (see diagram).

7. In each side piece drill a hole slightly larger than 3/16″ 1/4″ from the upper edge and 1/4″ from the end (rear).

8. In each end of the tailgate drill a 3/16″ hole 1/4″ from one edge (upper) and about 1/2″ deep. Center the holes on the ends.

9. Round off the inside lower edge of the tailgate.

10. Glue the sides of the box to the front end and attach the bottom.

11. Glue the 1 1/2″ piece to the bottom even with the back end, with the hole to the front and centered.

12. In one side of the box drill a 1/4″ hole 5/16″ deep, 1/2″ from the front end and lower edge of the bottom for the dumping lever.

13. Glue the front axle holder to the frame 1/4″ from the end and the rear holder 3/4″ from the end.

14. Glue the cab assembly to the frame letting it extend 1/4″ or so.

15. Round off the ends of the bumper and glue it to the frame.

16. At this point apply the finish.

17. Set the tailgate in place and drive in the 3/16″ pegs.

18. Set the box on the frame with the 1 1/2″ piece in the opening and the hole in line with the two outside holes.

19. Insert the dowel peg which can be glued fast or held in place by a piece of round toothpick or applicator stick driven into a hole made for it.

20. Glue the dumping lever in the hole.

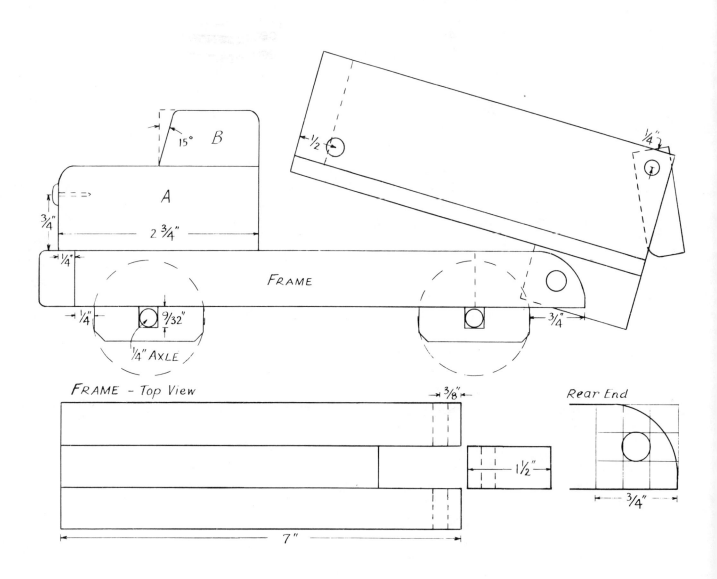

ROCK HAULER

Materials

3 pieces 3/4″ × 3/4″ × 8″——frame
1 piece 1 1/8″ × 3 1/2″ × 2 3/4″——A ⎫
1 piece 3/4″ × 3 1/2″ × 1 3/8″——B ⎬ cab and hood
1 piece 1/2″ × 3/4″ × 3 3/4″——bumper——hardwood
3 pieces 7/16″ × 1 1/2″ × 2 1/4″——axle holders
1 piece 7/16″ × 1 7/8″ × 3 1/2″——front end ⎫
2 pieces 7/16″ × 1 7/8″ × 6″——sides ⎬ box
1 piece 1/4″ × 4 3/8″ × 6″——bottom——plywood ⎭
1 piece 1/4″ × 4 3/8″ × 1 1/4″——C——plywood
1 piece 3/8″ dowel 3/4″ long——dumping lever
1 piece 1/4″ dowel 2 1/2″ long——peg
1 piece 1/4″ dowel 3 1/2″ long——front axle
2 pieces 1/4″ dowel 4 1/2″ long——rear axles
4 pieces 3/16″ dowel 1/2″ long——pegs
2 furniture nails——headlights
10   1 1/2″ wheels

Construction

1. Round off the top edge of one end (front) of the A piece and sand the upper surface. Saw off one end (front) of the B piece at a 15-degree angle. Glue B to A and round off the rear edge of B.

2. Drive in the headlights about 3/8″ in from the side edges and 3/4″ up from the lower edge.

3. Make the axle holders (see page 7). Cut a groove about 9/32″ × 9/32″ lengthwise in the upper surface of each axle holder. The groove should be equidistant from the side edges.

4. Drill a hole a little larger than 1/4″ in each frame piece 3/8″ from one end and centered. Or, in a piece of wood 3/4″ × 2 5/8″ or so, drill the hole crosswise 3/8″ from one end. Then cut the piece into 3/4″ strips.

5. Saw off a 1 1/2″ piece from one frame piece where the hole was drilled. Save this piece.

6. Glue the three pieces together with the end of the shorter middle piece even with the front ends of the side pieces. Be certain that the holes are opposite each other. Round off the ends of the outside pieces (see diagram).

7. Shape the sides of the box as shown in the diagram.

8. Glue the sides to the end and glue on the bottom. To strengthen the box, drive the 3/16″ dowel pegs in holes drilled through the bottom and into the sides about 1″ from the rear end.

9. Round off two corners (front) of the C piece. Glue it to the end and sides of the box. Drill 3/16″ holes 1/4″ deep, 1″ from the side edges for the 3/16″ pegs.

10. Glue the 1 1/2″ piece to the bottom of the box even with the rear end and centered. The hole should be to the front.

11. In the left side of the box drill a 3/8″ hole, 1/2″ from the front end and lower edge for the dumping lever. Insert the lever.

12. Glue the front axle holder to the frame 1/4″ from the end. Glue one rear holder in place 3/4″ from the end and the other holder 1/8″ in front of it.

13. Glue the cab assembly to the frame letting it extend 1/4″ beyond the end.

14. Round off the ends of the bumper and glue it to the frame.

15. At this point apply the finish.

16. Set the box on the frame with the 1 1/2″ piece in the opening and the hole in line with the other holes. Insert the dowel peg, which can be glued fast or held in place by a piece of round toothpick or applicator stick driven into a hole drilled for it.

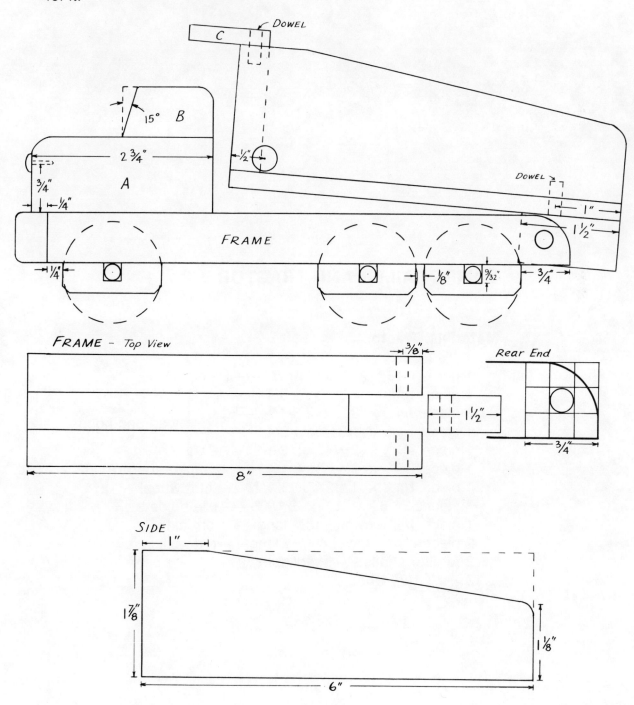

DUMP TRAILER AND TRACTOR

Materials: Tractor

1 piece 7/16″ × 2 1/4″ × 7″——frame
1 piece 1 1/8″ × 3″ × 2 3/4″——A
1 piece 3/4″ × 3″ × 2 3/4″——B
1 piece 1 1/8″ × 3″ × 1 3/4″——C } cab and hood
1 piece 1/4″ × 2 1/4″ × 2 1/2″——D
1 piece 1/2″ × 3/4″ × 3 1/4″——bumper—hardwood
1 piece 1/4″ × 1 1/2″ × 1 1/2″——fifth wheel
3 pieces 7/16″ × 1″ × 2 1/4″——axle holders
1 piece 1/4″ dowel 3 1/2″ long——front axle
2 pieces 1/4″ dowel 4 1/2″ long——rear axle
2 furniture nails——headlights
10   1 1/2″ wheels

Construction

1. With the saw blade tilted at 15 degrees saw off one end (front) of the C piece. Round off the upper back edge.

2. Glue A to B. Round off the top front edge of A and sand the upper surface. Glue C to A (see diagram).

3. Drive in the headlights 1 1/2" from the lower edge and 3/8" from the side edges.

4. In the center of each axle holder cut a 9/32" × 9/32" groove lengthwise.

5. Glue the front axle holder to the frame 3/8" from the end. Glue one rear holder to the frame 1/8" from the end and the other holder 3/4" from it or 1 7/8" from the end.

6. Glue the D piece to the frame even with the front end. This piece will support the cab assembly.

7. Glue the cab assembly to D letting it extend 1/4" beyond the end of the frame.

8. Round off the ends of the bumper and glue it to the frame.

9. Shape the fifth wheel and glue it to the frame 3/4" from the end and centered.

10. Through the center of the fifth wheel and frame, drill a 13/32" hole.

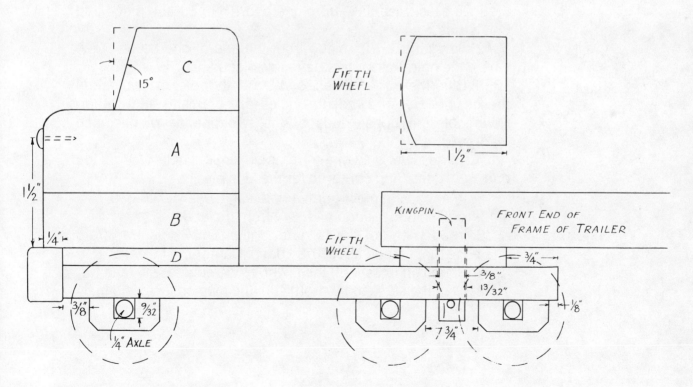

Materials: Trailer

3 pieces 3/4" × 3/4" × 7 1/4"——frame
2 pieces 7/16" × 1 3/4" × 2 5/8"——front end
    and tailgate
2 pieces 7/16" × 1 3/4" × 8"——sides } box
1 piece 1/4" × 3 1/2" × 8"——bottom
2 pieces 3/4" × 1 1/4" × 2 1/4"——x } axle holder
1 piece 7/16" × 7/8" × 2 1/4"——y
1 piece 3/8" dowel 3/4" long——dumping lever
1 piece 3/8" dowel 1 3/8" long——king pin
1 piece 1/4" dowel 2 3/4" long——peg
2 pieces 1/4" dowel 4 1/2" long——axles
2 pieces 3/16" dowel 1" long——tailgate pegs
1 piece 1/8" dowel 5/8" long——peg
8   1 1/2" wheels

Construction

1. In each frame piece drill a 17/64" hole 3/8" from one end and centered. Or, in a piece of wood 3/4" × 2 5/8" or so, drill the hole crosswise 3/8" from one end. Then cut the piece into 3/4" strips.

2. Saw off a 1 1/2" piece from the end of one frame piece where the hole was drilled. Save this piece.

3. Glue the three pieces together with the shorter piece in the middle. Be sure that the holes are opposite each other. Round off the upper ends of the two outside pieces (see diagram).

4. In the lower side of the frame drill a 3/8" hole 1" from the end, 3/8" deep, and centered for the king pin.

5. In each side piece, drill a hole slightly larger than 3/16", 1/4" from the upper edge and 1/4" from the end (rear).

6. In each end of the tailgate, drill a 3/16" hole 1/4" from one edge (upper) and about 1/2" deep. Center the holes.

7. Round off or saw off the lower inside edge of the tailgate.

8. Glue the sides to the front end and glue on the bottom.

9. Glue the 1 1/2″ piece to the bottom even with the back end and centered. The hole in the piece should be to the front.

10. In one side of the box, drill a 3/8″ hole 5/16″ deep, 1/2″ from the front end and lower edge for the dumping lever.

11. Make the axle holder (see page 7). Drill 9/32″ holes lengthwise through each x piece 3/8″ from the lower edge and centered.

12. Glue the axle holder to the frame 3/4″ from the rear end.

13. Apply the finish to the trailer and tractor at this point.

14. Set the tailgate in place and drive in the pegs.

15. Set the box on the frame with the 1 1/2″ piece in the opening and the hole in line with the other holes. Insert the dowel peg, which can be glued in or made secure by a piece of round toothpick or applicator stick put into a hole drilled for it.

16. Drill a 1/8″ hole 1/4″ from one end of the king pin and insert the 1/8″ dowel peg.

17. Glue the dumping lever in the hole.

18. Put glue in the hole in the frame. Insert the king pin up through the tractor frame and the fifth wheel into the hole. The trailer should ride on the fifth wheel. See tractor diagram.

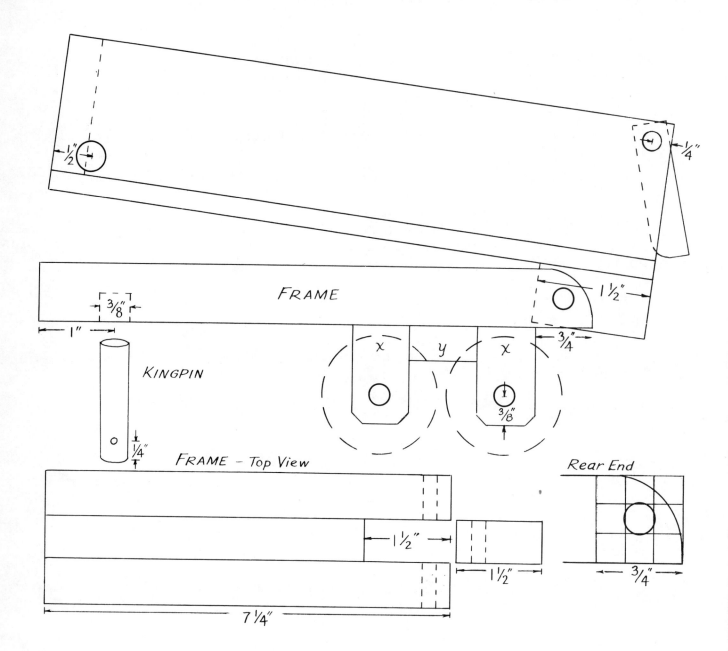

FRAME

$\frac{1}{2}$" $\frac{1}{4}$"

$\frac{3}{8}$"

1"

$1\frac{1}{2}$"

$\frac{3}{4}$"

KINGPIN

x   y   x

$\frac{3}{8}$"

$\frac{1}{4}$"

FRAME – Top View

Rear End

$1\frac{1}{2}$"

$1\frac{1}{2}$"

$\frac{3}{4}$"

$7\frac{1}{4}$"

ROAD GRADER

Materials

1 piece 7/16" × 2" × 9 1/2"——frame
1 piece 1 1/8" × 2" × 2 1/4"——engine
1 piece 7/16" × 1 1/2" × 2 1/4"——back ⎤
2 pieces 1/4" × 1 1/4" × 2 1/4"——sides ⎟
1 piece 1/4" × 1 1/2" × 2"——roof ⎬ cab
1 piece 3/4" × 3/4" × 1 1/2"——seat ⎦
1 piece 3/4" × 1 1/4" × 2"——front axle holder
2 pieces 3/4" × 1 1/4" × 2"——x ⎤ rear axle holder
1 piece 3/4" × 7/8" × 2"——y ⎦
1 piece 1/2" dowel 3" long——post ⎤
1 piece 1/4" dowel 5 1/4" ⎟
    long——lever ⎬ steering mechanism
1 piece 1/8" dowel 1/2" long——peg ⎦
1 piece 1/8" × 3/4" × 4"——blade— ⎤
    plywood ⎟
1 piece 7/16" × 3/4" × 1"——blade ⎬ blade assembly
    holder ⎟
1 piece 1/4" dowel 1 1/2" long ⎟
1 piece 7/16" × 1/2" × 1"——handle ⎦
1 piece 1/4" dowel 3 1/4" long——front axle
2 pieces 1/4" dowel 4 1/4" long——rear axles
10 1 1/2" wheels

Construction

1. In one end (front) of the frame, drill a hole slightly larger than 1/2"–3/4" from the end and centered. The steering post should turn in this hole.

2. Then 4 3/4" from the same end, drill a 1/4" hole equidistant from the side edges.

3. Round off the front corners of the frame.

4. Make the axle holders (see page 7). The 3/4" sides of y should be against the x pieces. Drill 17/64" holes lengthwise through each x piece and the front holder 3/8" from the lower edges and centered.

5. Glue the rear axle holder to the frame 1/4" from the end.

6. In the center of the front axle holder drill a 1/2" hole 1/2" in depth. Glue the steering post in this hole.

7. Glue the sides of the cab to the back and put on the roof.

8. Glue the engine to the frame even with the rear end. Glue the cab to the frame and engine. Put in the seat.

9. Drill a 1/8" hole partway through the steering post. To locate this hole set the post into the frame and make a mark so that the center of the hole is an 1/8" or so above the frame.

10. Drill a 1/4" hole through the post 1/2" from the upper end for the steering lever.

11. Put the steering post up through the frame and drive in the 1/8" peg. Insert the steering lever.

12. Cut an 1/8" groove 3/16" in depth lengthwise in the center of the blade holder. In the center of the top of the holder drill a 1/4" hole 3/16" deep. Glue the dowel in the hole and the blade in the groove. Drill a 1/4" hole partway through the center of the handle.

13. Put the dowel of the blade assembly up through the hole in the frame and glue on the handle. The dowel should fit snugly in the hole yet loose enough so that the blade can be turned or moved up and down.

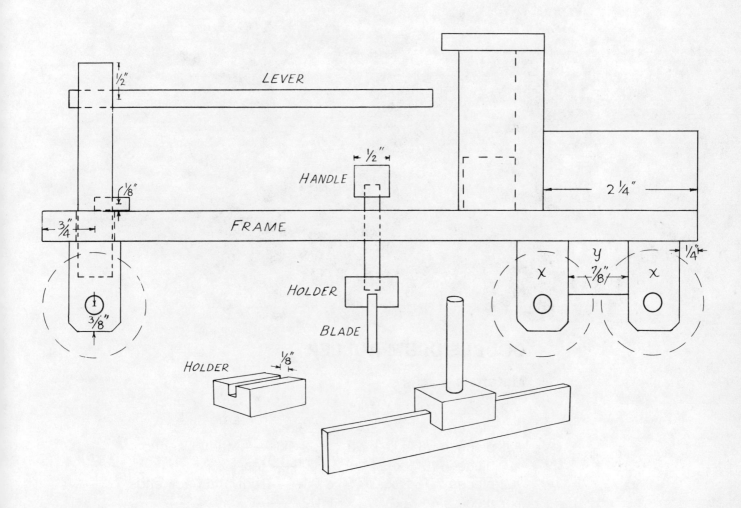

LEVER

½"

⅛"

¾"

FRAME

½"

HANDLE

2¼"

HOLDER

BLADE

y

⅞"

x   x

¼"

⅜"

HOLDER

⅛"

DOUBLE DRUM ROLLER

Materials

2 pieces 7/16″ × 3/4″ × 6 1/2″ } frame
2 pieces 7/16″ × 3/4″ × 2 3/8″ } frame
1 piece 1 1/8″ × 1 1/2″ × 2 3/8″——center section
1 piece 7/16″ × 2″ × 6 1/2″——top
2 pieces 7/16″ × 3/4″ × 2″——front and back ends
1 piece 3/4″ × 3/4″ × 1 1/2″——A
1 piece 7/16″——3/4″ × 1/2″——bottom } seat
1 piece 1/4″ × 3/4″ × 1″——back } seat
2 cylinders 2″ in diameter by 2 1/4″ long——drums
2 pieces 1/4″ dowel 3 3/8″ long——axles
4 pieces 1/4″ dowel 1″ long——pegs
1 piece 3/16″ dowel 1″ long——steering wheel shaft
1   3/4″ wheel——steering wheel

The drums can be made on a lathe or by cutting out discs, 2″ in diameter, with a hole saw or a single-wing hole cutter. Three discs cut from 3/4″ stock or two from 1 1/8″ stock, when glued together, will make drums 2 1/4″ long. If the drums are longer or shorter than 2 1/4″, adjustments can readily be made in the length of the end pieces and center piece.

96

Construction

1. In each side piece of the frame drill a hole slightly larger than 1/4", 1 5/8" from either end and centered. Also drill a 1/4" hole in the center of each piece.

2. Glue the end pieces between the side pieces to make the frame.

3. Glue the center section in place even with the lower edges of the side pieces. Drill 1/4" holes through the center holes in the side frame pieces into the center section about 5/8" in depth. Drive in the pegs.

4. Glue the front and back end pieces to the top even with the ends. Center this assembly on the frame and glue in place.

5. Drill two 1/4" holes about 5/8" deep through the top into the center piece. Locate the holes 3 1/4" from either end and 1/2" from the side edges. Drive in the pegs.

6. Round off two top side edges of the A piece (see diagram). In the rear surface drill a 3/16" hole for the steering shaft at an angle downward 1/4" from the upper edge and equidistant from the ends.

7. Fasten the wheel on the shaft and insert the shaft into the hole in A. Glue this assembly to the top 2 1/4" from one end and centered.

8. Glue the seat in place about 5/8" from the A piece.

9. Apply the finish at this point.

10. Drill holes in the drums large enough so they will revolve easily on the 1/4" axles. Install the drums.

11. Drill a hole through the underside of the frame into each axle for a small dowel or peg. A piece of round toothpick or applicator stick will do for this.

Front View

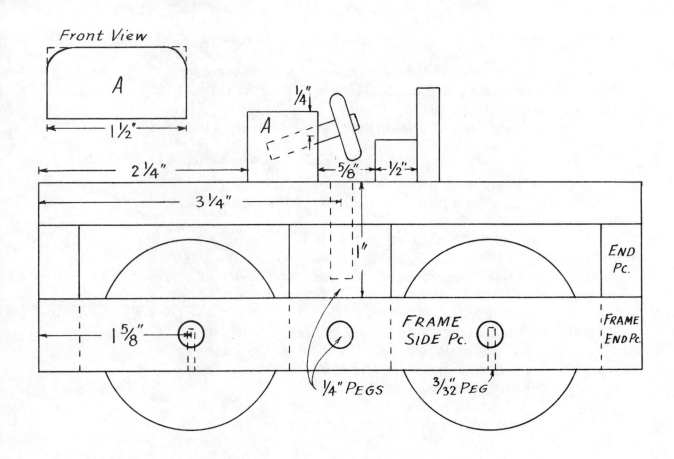

A

1½"

¼"

A

2¼"

5⁄8" ½"

3¼"

1"

END
Pc.

1⅝"

FRAME
SIDE Pc.

FRAME
END Pc.

¼" PEGS

3⁄32 PEG

6
On the Railroad

Freight Train
Water Tank
Passenger Train
Suburban Station

Once you start making a train, it can be hard to stop. The freight train described here includes many of the cars most commonly seen. If only one of each type car is made, the completed train will be about 4 feet long. The cars on the passenger train are pretty much the same, and the length of the train will depend only on the number of cars you choose to make. The suburban station is very simple in design, intended to reflect those that serve as shelters for waiting passengers. You may want to design a more elaborate station with a ticket office, waiting room, and outside platform.

FREIGHT TRAIN

Materials: Engine

1 piece 7/16″ × 1 1/2″ × 7 1/2″——frame
1 piece 1 1/8″ × 1 3/8″ × 6 1/2″——A ⎫
1 piece 7/16″ × 1 3/8″ × 5 1/4″——B ⎬ boiler
1 piece 5/8″ × 1 3/8″ × 1 1/2″——cab roof
1 piece 1/2″ dowel 3/4″ long——smokestack
4 pieces 3/16″ dowel 2 3/8″ long——axles
8   1 1/4″ wheels
2 furniture nails (or use dowel buttons 1/2″ diameter)——
    domes
1 small furniture nail——headlight
1 piece 3/16″ × 1/2″ × 3 1/2″ ⎫ coupler—hardwood
1 piece 1/4″ dowel 3/4″ long   ⎬ or 3/16″ plywood

Construction

1. Mark the center point at one end of the frame. Set the miter gauge at 60 degrees and saw off both corners to this point. Tilt the saw to about 45 degrees and saw off the upper side of this pointed end.

2. In the upper surface of the frame make a groove lengthwise about 4″ long, 1/2″ wide, and 3/16″ in depth. If a dado saw is not available, make several cuts with the regular saw.

3. In the coupler bar drill a 1/4″ hole 3/8″ from one end and centered. Round off this end and glue the bar in the groove. It should extend about 1″ beyond the end of the frame.

4. Through one side of the frame drill four 7/32″ holes for the axles. Locate the first hole 1 1/2″ from the back end, and the other three holes 1 1/2″ apart. If screws are used for axles instead of dowels, drill pilot holes for them in each side of the frame.

5. In each 1 1/8″ side of the A piece make a narrow saw cut 1 1/4″ from one end (rear) and about 1/8″ deep. Also drill a 1/4″ hole about 1/4″ in depth in each side midway between the saw cut and the end, 1/4″ from the upper surface.

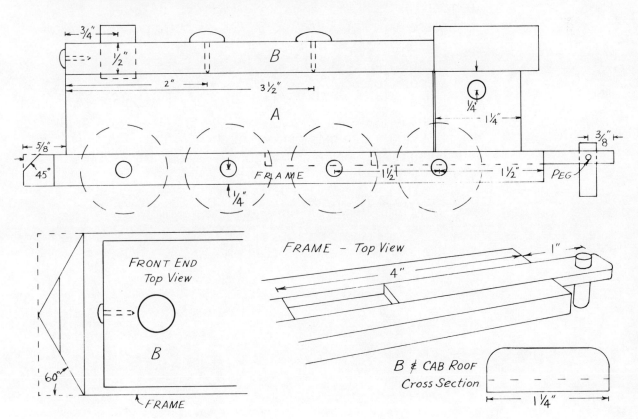

6. Glue B to A even with the front end.

7. Drill a 1/2" hole 3/4" from the front end of the boiler about 1/2" deep for the smokestack. Indicate the location of the domes if furniture nails are used. Drill holes if using dowel buttons. The domes should be 2" and 3 1/2" from the front end.

8. Round off the side edges of the boiler and the cab roof. A moulding cutter, if available, is good for this.

9. Sand the boiler and glue it to the frame 5/8" back from the end of the cowcatcher.

10. Glue the smokestack in place and install the domes.

11. Glue on the cab roof.

12. Drive the dowel peg into the hole in the coupler bar. To make sure that the peg does not come out, drill a hole through one side of the bar and the peg. Insert a piece of round toothpick or applicator stick. A no. 44 drill is good for this.

13. Drive in the headlight.

Materials: Cars

Tender
    1 piece 7/16" × 1 1/2" × 3 1/2"——bottom
    2 pieces 7/16" × 1 1/8" × 1"——ends
    2 pieces 1/4" × 1 1/8" × 3 1/2"——sides
    1 piece 3/16" × 1/2" × 5 1/2"——bar ⎤
    1 piece 3/16" × 1/2" × 1"——A ⎥ coupler—hardwood
    1 piece 1/4" dowel 3/4" ⎥ or plywood
        long (or use axle pin)——hitch ⎦
    2 pieces 3/16" dowel 2 1/4" long——axles
    4   1" wheels

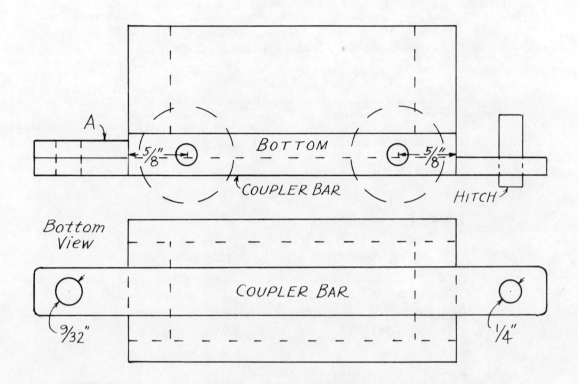

A

5/8"   BOTTOM   5/8"

COUPLER BAR

HITCH

Bottom
View

COUPLER BAR

9/32"   1/4"

Box Car
    2 pieces 1/4″ × 1 1/8″ × 4 1/2″——sides
    2 pieces 7/16″ × 1 1/8″ × 1″——ends
    2 pieces 1/32″ × 3/4″ × 1 1/8″——doors
    1 piece 1/4″ × 1 1/2″ × 4 1/2″
    1 piece 1/8″ × 15/16″ × 3 9/16″——underpiece } roof
    1 piece 1/16″ × 1/4″ × 4 1/2″——catwalk

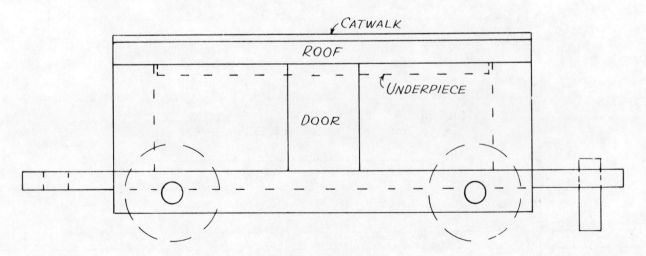

CATWALK

ROOF

UNDERPIECE

DOOR

Flat Car
Listed under additional materials, page 106

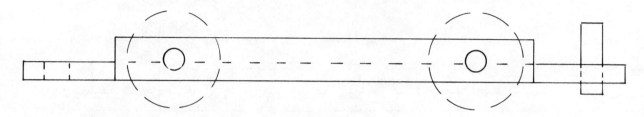

Cattle Car
6 pieces 1/8″ × 5/16″ × 4 1/2″——sides
2 pieces 7/16″ × 1 1/8″ × 1 1/4″——ends
2 pieces 1/32″ × 3/4″ × 1 1/8″——doors
1 piece 1/4″ × 1 1/2″ × 4 1/2″
1 piece 1/8″ × 1 3/16″ × 3 9/16″——underpiece } roof
1 piece 1/16″ × 1/4″ × 4 1/2″——catwalk

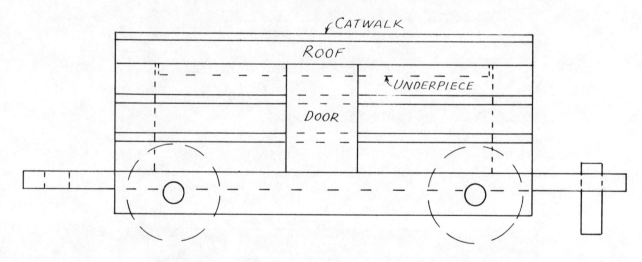

Gondola Car
2 pieces 1/4″ × 3/4″ × 4 1/2″——sides
2 pieces 7/16″ × 3/4″ × 1″——ends

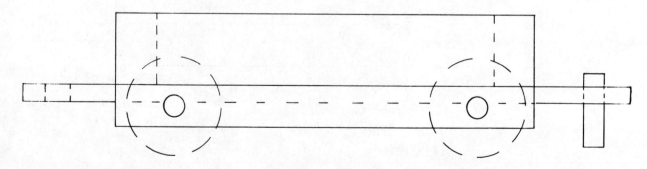

Lumber Car
8 pieces 3/16″ dowel 1″ long——stakes

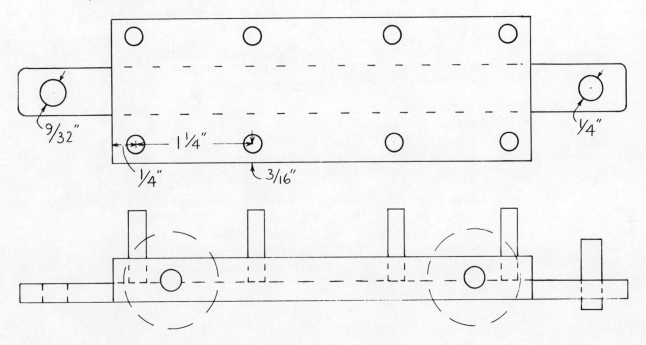

Tank Car
1 piece 1″ dowel 3 1/2″ long——tank
1 piece 1/2″ dowel 3/4″ long——hatch
1 piece 7/16″ × 1 1/4″ × 1 1/2″——for tank supports

TANK SUPPORTS

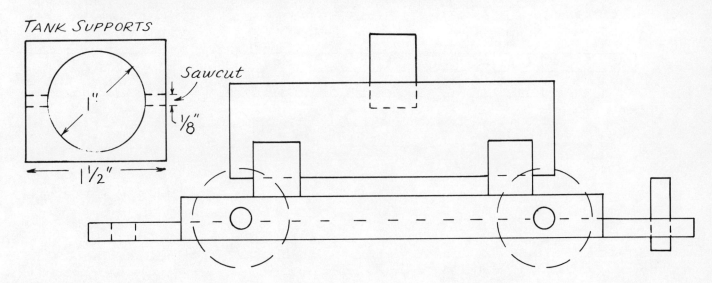

Additional materials for the six cars listed above

6 pieces 7/16″ × 1 1/2″ × 4 1/2″——bottoms
6 pieces 3/16″ × 1/2″ × 6 1/2″——bars
6 pieces 1/4″ dowel 3/4″ long (or use axle pins)——hitch } coupler—
12 pieces 3/16″ dowel 2 1/4″ long——axles } hardwood
24   1″ wheels   or plywood

Caboose

1 piece 7/16″ × 1 1/2″ × 3 1/2″——bottom
2 pieces 7/16″ × 3/4″ × 1″——ends
2 pieces 1/4″ × 3/4″ × 2 3/4″——sides
1 piece 1/4″ × 1 9/16″ × 3 1/2″
1 piece 1/8″ × 15/16″ × 1 13/16″——underpiece } roof
1 piece 7/16″ × 1 1/4″ × 3/4″——cupola
1 piece 3/16″ × 1/2″ × 4 1/2″——coupler bar
2 pieces 3/16″ dowel 2 1/4″ long——axles
4   1″ wheels

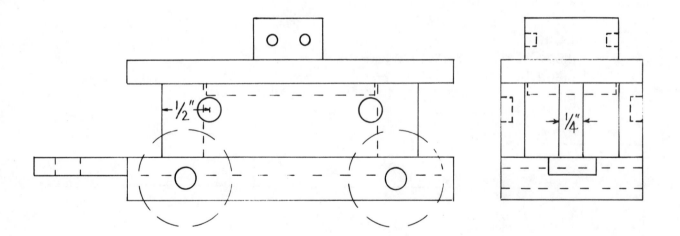

Construction

Instructions are given for making six cars in addition to the tender and caboose. The construction of the cars is similar. Any differences will be explained in each case. The illustrations show the correct location of the coupler bar and hitch in each car.

1. Through the center of each bottom piece, including the tender and caboose, cut a groove lengthwise 3/16″ deep and 1/2″ wide.

2. Make six coupler bars 6 1/2″ long for the cars, one 5 1/2″ long for the tender and one 4 1/2″ long for the caboose. Glue the A piece to one end of the bar for the tender. This piece is needed to provide better coupling due to the larger wheels on the engine.

3. Drill a 9/32″ hole 3/8″ from one end of each bar and centered. Drill the hole in the bar for the tender in the end where the A piece was glued on. Drill a 1/4″ hole for the hitch 3/8″ from the other end of each bar, except the bar for the caboose. Round off the ends where the holes were drilled.

4. Glue the coupler bars in the grooves in the bottoms. They should extend 1″ at each end with the exception of the bar for the caboose which extends only at the front end. The bars should be even with the surface of the bottoms.

5. Drill 7/32″ holes for the axles crosswise through the bottom pieces. Locate the holes 5/8″ from either end and centered. If screws are used for axles drill pilot holes for them instead.

6. Glue the sides to the ends of the tender, box car, and gondola car.

7. Glue the box for the tender to the bottom with the coupler bar in the underside. The 9/32″ hole should be to the front. The hitch should extend upward.

8. The coupler bar for the box car should be in the upper surface of the bottom when gluing on the box. The hitch should extend downward with the 9/32″ hole to the front. Glue the doors on equidistant from the ends. Center the underpiece on the roof and glue it fast. Glue the catwalk to the center of the roof.

9. The coupler bar for the flat car should be in the underside of the bottom. When the bar is in the underside, the hitch extends upward. When in the upper side, the hitch extends downward.

10. When assembling the cattle car, glue the ends to the bottom first. Then glue on the lower and upper side pieces and the middle one last. Glue the doors on equidistant from the ends. Center the underpiece on the roof and glue in place. Glue the catwalk to the center of the roof. The coupler bar should be in the upper side of the bottom.

11. Along each side of the bottom of the lumber car that does not have the groove in it, drill four 3/16″ holes about 1/4″ deep for the stakes. Locate the holes 3/16″ from the side edges with the end holes 1/4″ from the ends and the other holes 1 1/2″ from the ends.

12. Glue the box for the gondola car to the bottom. The coupler bar should be in the upper side.

13. Midway between the ends of the tank drill a 1/2″ hole about 1/4″ deep for the hatch. Glue the dowel in the hole. Drill a 1″ hole through the center of the tank support piece and saw it in half. Glue the supports to the bottom 3/4″ from either end. The coupler bar should be in the underside.

14. In each side piece for the caboose drill two 1/4″ holes about 1/8″ deep, 1/2″ from the ends, and 1/4″ from the upper edge. Center the underpiece on the roof and glue in place. Drill two 1/8″ holes 1/8″ deep in each 3/4″ side of the cupola and glue it to the center of the roof. In the center of the outside surfaces of each end piece, make vertical grooves 1/4″ wide and 1/8″ deep for the doorways. Assemble the caboose.

15. When there are an odd number of cars in the train, counting the tender, the coupler bar of the caboose should be in the upper side of the bottom. If an even number of cars caboose coupler bar should be in the underside. Decide how many cars will be in the train before assembling the caboose.

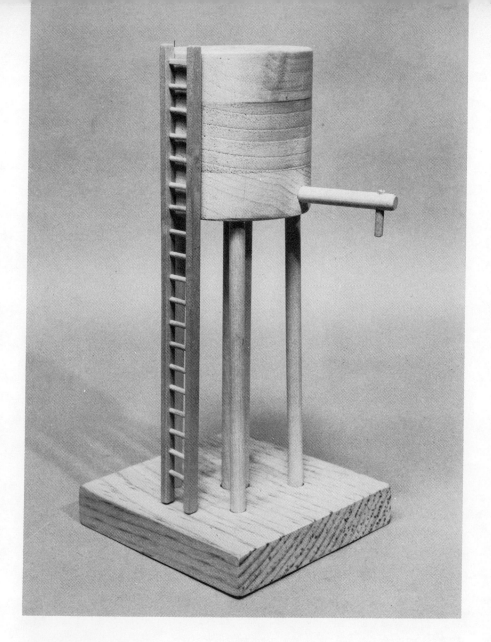

WATER TANK

Materials

    1 cylinder about 2 1/2″ in diameter and 2 1/2″ long——tank
    1 piece 1/4″ dowel 2″ long   ⎫
    1 piece 1/8″ dowel 3/4″ long ⎬ spout
    4 pieces 1/4″ dowel 6″ long   ⎫
    1 piece 1/2″ dowel 6″ long   ⎬ tank supports
    1 piece 3/4″ × 4″ × 4″——base
    2 pieces 1/8″ × 3/16″ × 7 1/2″——rails   ⎫
19 pieces 3/32″ dowel (applicator sticks) 5/8″ ⎬ ladder
       long——rungs

Construction

1. This is a project for a toymaker with a lathe or who has a friend with one. The size of the tank is a suggested one and may vary at the discretion of the toymaker.

2. On one flat end of the cylinder (bottom of tank) drill four 1/4″ holes about 1/2″ in depth equally spaced about 1/4″ in from the edge. Also in the bottom of the tank drill a 1/2″ hole in the center about 1/2″ deep.

3. On the curved side drill a 1/4″ hole 1/4″ up from the bottom for the spout.

4. Drive the dowel supports into the holes in the bottom of the tank.

5. Mark the centerpoint on the base and drill a 1/2″ hole about 1/2″ deep. Insert the 1/2″ dowel into this hole and set the tank on it. Mark the location for the four 1/4″ holes which should be about 1/2″ deep.

6. Put glue into the holes and set the tank in place.

7. Drill a 1/8″ hole 1/4″ from one end of the spout. Drive in the 1/8″ dowel. Insert the spout into the hole in the tank.

8. To make the rails for the ladder, draw parallel lines 3/8″ apart on a piece of 1/8″ plywood. Use the try square as a guide. Locate the first line 1/2″ from one end, which will be the lower end of the ladder. Saw off two strips 3/16″ wide for the rails.

9. In the center of each line drill a hole about 3/32″ deep for the rungs. A no. 44 drill is just right for this.

10. Put a little glue on one end of each rung and insert it into one rail. Again apply glue and fit the rungs into the other rail.

11. Glue the ladder to the side of the tank.

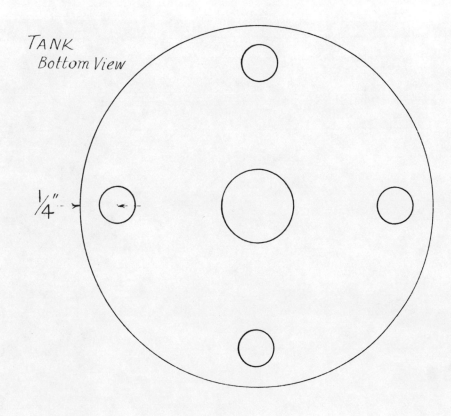

TANK
Bottom View

$\frac{1}{4}$"

MATERIAL FOR RAILS

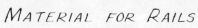

Grain

$\frac{1}{2}$ $\frac{3}{8}$

$\frac{3}{16}$"

RAIL

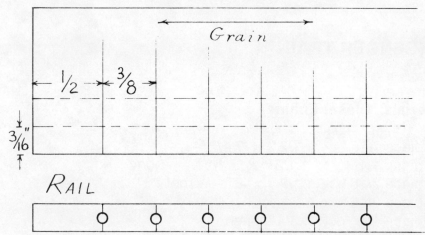

PASSENGER TRAIN

Materials: Diesel Engine

1 piece 7/16″ × 1 1/2″ × 7 1/2″——frame
1 piece 1 1/8″ × 1 1/2″ × 7 1/2″——body
1 piece 7/16″ × 1 1/2″ × 6″——roof
1 piece 3/16″ × 1/2″ × 3 1/2″ ⎫
1 piece 1/4″ dowel 3/4″ long ⎭ coupler
4 pieces 3/16″ dowel 2 1/8″ long——axles
8   1″ wheels
1 small furniture nail——headlight

Construction

1. In each 1 1/8″ side of the engine body indicate the doors by making narrow parallel saw cuts 3/8″ apart and 1/8″ in depth. The saw cuts should be about 2 1/2″ and 5″ from the rear end. Drill an 1/8″ hole about 1/4″ deep between each pair of saw cuts 1/4″ from the upper surface. Also drill a similar hole 3/4″ from the rear end (see diagram).

2. Sand the upper surface of the body.

3. Shape the front end of the roof piece by marking the midpoint on one end. Set the miter gauge at 60 degrees and tilt the saw at 30 degrees. Saw to the point. Make three or four shallow saw cuts to reach the point. Change the miter gauge to 60 degrees on the other side of center and shape the other side. Round off the side edges of the roof.

4. In the center of the upper surface of the frame make a 1/2″ groove lengthwise 3/16″ in depth and 4″ long. In the coupler bar drill a 1/4″ hole 3/8″ from one end. Round off the end.

5. Glue the bar in the groove allowing it to extend 1″.

6. Drill four 7/32″ holes crosswise through one side edge of the frame for the axles. Locate the holes 1″, 2 1/8″, 5″, and 6 1/8″ from the rear end. If screws are used for axles, drill pilot holes for them in each side of the frame.

7. Glue the body to the frame and round off the front side corners.

8. Glue the roof on.

9. Drive the dowel into the coupler bar. It may be made more secure by drilling a small hole through the side edge of the bar and the dowel and inserting a piece of round toothpick or applicator stick.

10. Install the headlight.

11. Apply the finish.

12. Mount the wheels.

Top View

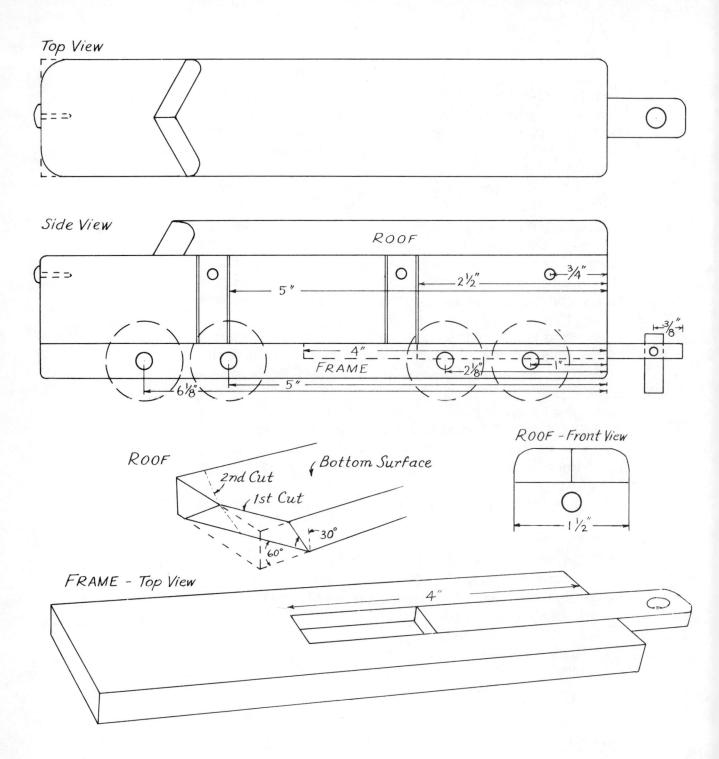

Side View

ROOF

5"

2½"

¾"

⅜"

4"

FRAME

2⅛"

1"

6⅛"

5"

ROOF

2nd Cut

1st Cut

Bottom Surface

30°

60°

ROOF - Front View

1½"

FRAME - Top View

4"

Materials: Passenger Car

1 piece 7/16″ × 1 1/2″ × 7 1/2″——bottom or floor
2 pieces 7/16″ × 1 1/8″ × 1″——ends ⎫
2 pieces 1/4″ × 1 1/8″ × 6″——sides ⎬ body
2 pieces 3/4″ × 1 1/2″ × 1 1/8″——A—vestibules
1 piece 7/16″ × 1 1/2″ × 7 1/2″——roof
1 piece 1/8″ × 15/16″ × 5 1/16″——roof underpiece
1 piece 1/4″ × 3/4″ × 7 1/2″——top piece—roof
1 piece 3/16″ × 1/2″ × 9 1/2″——bar ⎫
1 piece 1/4″ dowel 3/4″ long ⎬ coupler
4 pieces 3/16″ dowel 2 1/8″ long——axles
8   1″ wheels

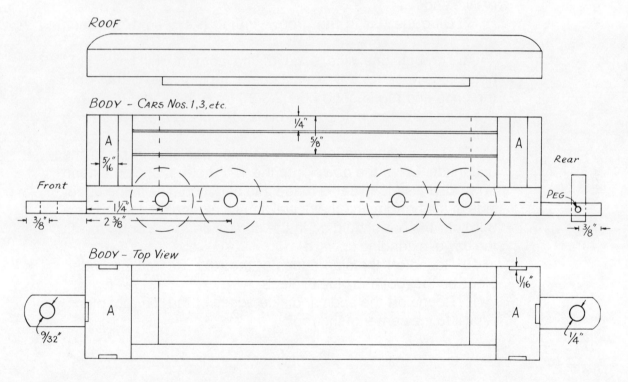

Roof

Body - Cars Nos. 1, 3, etc.

Body - Top View

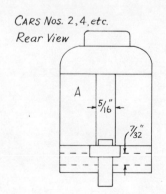

Cars Nos. 2, 4, etc.
Rear View

Construction

1. In each side piece make narrow saw cuts lengthwise 1/4″ and 5/8″ from the upper edge to represent windows.

2. Glue the sides to the ends.

3. In the center of three sides of the vestibules make a groove lengthwise 5/16″ wide and about 1/16″ in depth to represent doorways.

4. Glue the A pieces to the ends of the car body.

5. In the center of the bottom cut a groove lengthwise 3/16″ deep and 1/2″ wide for the coupler bar.

6. Drill a 9/32″ hole 3/8″ from one end of the coupler bar and a 1/4″ hole the same distance from the other end. Round off the ends.

7. Glue the bar in the groove letting it extend 1″ at each end.

8. Through one side edge of the bottom drill four 7/32″ holes crosswise for the axles. Locate the first hole 1 1/4″ from the ends and the second hole 2 3/8″ from the ends. If screws are used for axles instead of dowels, drill pilot holes for them in each side edge.

9. Glue on the bottom. The coupler bar should be in the underside. Drive the dowel into the 1/4″ hole. It should extend upward. If a second car is made, the bar should be in the upper side of the bottom and the dowel should extend downward. In a third car the bar should be in the underside of the bottom with the dowel extending upward.

10. Round off the side edges of the roof. Center the underpiece on the roof and glue in place.

11. Round off the ends and side edges of the top roof piece. Glue it to the center of the roof.

116

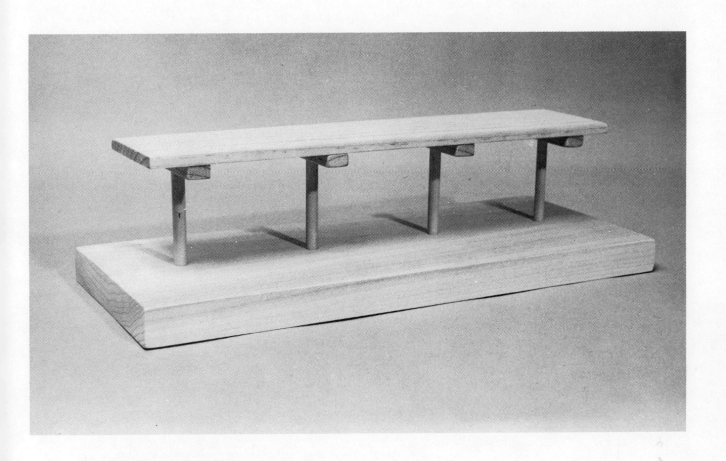

SUBURBAN STATION

Materials

1 piece 3/4″ × 5″ × 12″——platform
1 piece 1/4″ × 2 1/2″ × 11″——roof
4 pieces 1/4″ × 1/2″ × 2 1/2″——roof supports
4 pieces 1/4″ dowel 2 3/4″ long——posts

Construction

1. Drill four 1/4″ holes 1/2″ deep in the platform. Locate the end holes 1 1/2″ from the ends of the platform and midway between the side edges. The other two holes should be 4 1/2″ from the ends.

2. In the center of each roof support drill a 1/4″ hole. Glue two supports to the underside of the roof 3/4″ in from the ends and the other two 3 3/4″ from the ends. The centers of the holes should be 3″ apart to conform to the holes in the platform.

3. Set the posts into the platform and install the roof.

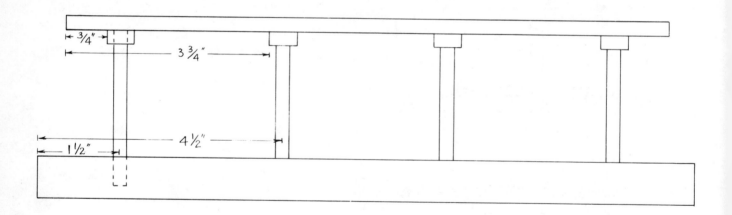

7
On the Water

Tugboat
Speedboat
Houseboat
Pontoon Boats
Freighter

In this set are boats for use as floor toys and for playing with in the water. One pontoon boat has wheels, as does the freighter, and both are designed for floor play. The other boats, when finished with a material recommended for boats, such as Valspar, can be used in the bathtub or pool.

TUGBOAT

Materials

 1 piece 1 3/4″ × 2 3/4″ × 6″——hull
 1 piece 3/4″ × 1 3/4″ × 3 1/4″——deckhouse
 1 piece 3/4″ × 1 1/4″ × 1 1/4″——pilothouse
 1 piece 3/4″ dowel 1 1/2″ long——smokestack
 2 pieces 3/16″ dowel 3/4″ long——bitts
 1 piece 1 1/8″ × 2 1/2″ × 6″ ⎫
 1 piece 3/4″ × 1 1/2″ × 2″   ⎬ jig
           ⎭

Construction

1. To obtain the tapered shape of the hull, a jig will have to be made to guide the stock through the saw. Make the jig as shown in the diagram. The hull should be about 1 1/2" thick at the prow and 3/4" at the stern.

2. On the hull draw lines as in the diagram. A 6" saucer is good for this. Also draw a line down the center of the front end of the hull to serve as a guide for the sharp edge of the prow.

3. In the deckhouse drill a 3/4" hole about 5/8" deep 1" from one end and centered for the smokestack. Also drill three 1/4" holes in each side about 1/2" deep. Locate the holes 3/4" from either end and one in the center. Round off the ends.

4. Round off one end (front) of the pilot house.

5. Glue the pilothouse to the deckhouse 1/4" from the front end and centered. Use a waterproof glue. Glue this assembly to the hull 1 1/2" from the prow and equidistant from the side edges.

6. Install the smokestack.

7. Drill 3/16" holes 3/8" deep 1/2" from either end for the bitts.

8. Use a finish recommended for boats.

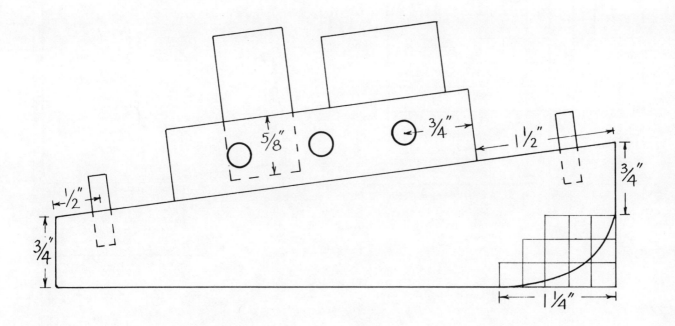

HULL

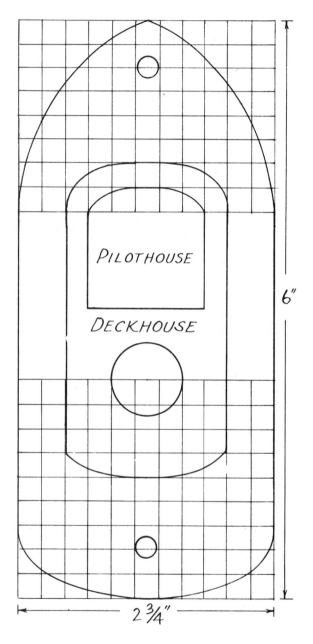

PILOTHOUSE

DECKHOUSE

2 3/4"

6"

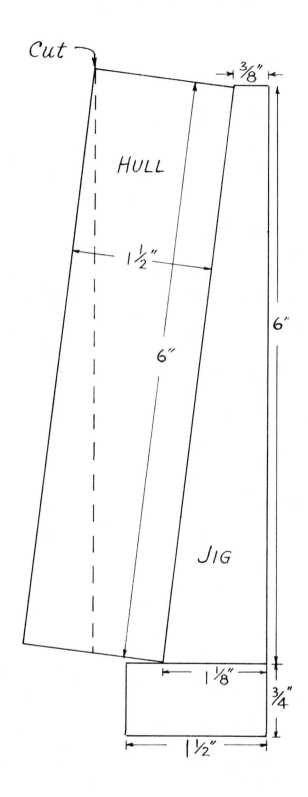

Cut

HULL

3/8"

1 1/2"

6"

6"

JIG

1 1/8"

3/4"

1 1/2"

122

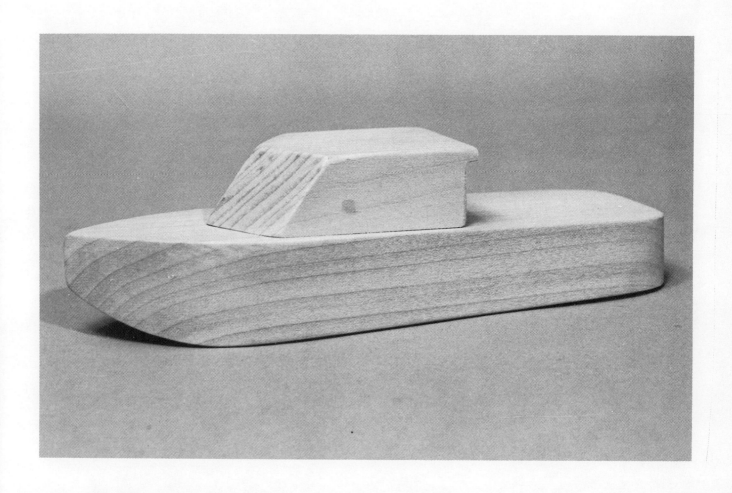

SPEED BOAT

Materials

    1 piece 1 1/8″ × 2″ × 6″——hull
    1 piece 3/4″ × 1 3/4″ × 2 1/2″——cabin
    1 piece 1 1/8″ × 2 1/2″ × 5 1/4″ ⎫
    1 piece 3/4″ × 1 1/2″ × 1 5/8″ ⎬ jig

Construction

1. A jig will be needed to obtain the shape of the hull. Using the diagram as a guide, make the jig. The hull should be about 1″ thick at the prow, before being shaped, and 5/8″ at the stern.

2. Shape the hull as shown in the diagram.

3. Form the back end of the cabin by making one or more saw cuts to a depth of 5/8″ (see diagram).

4. Shape the front end of the cabin by marking the midpoint on the upper surface at the end. Set the miter gauge at 60 degrees and tilt the saw blade at 30 degrees. With the upper surface of the cabin on the saw table saw to the point marked. Change the miter gauge to 60 degrees on the other side of center and shape the other side.

5. Using a waterproof glue, fasten the cabin to the hull about 1 1/4″ from the prow. A no. 6—1 1/2″ flathead brass screw may be driven through the hull into the cabin to make sure that it does not come off when in the water.

6. Finish with a material recommended for boats.

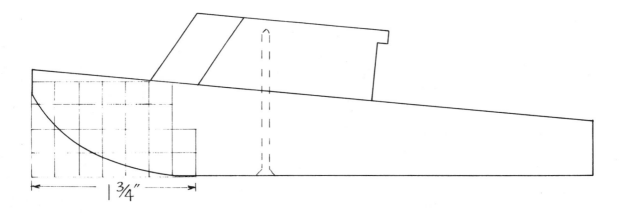

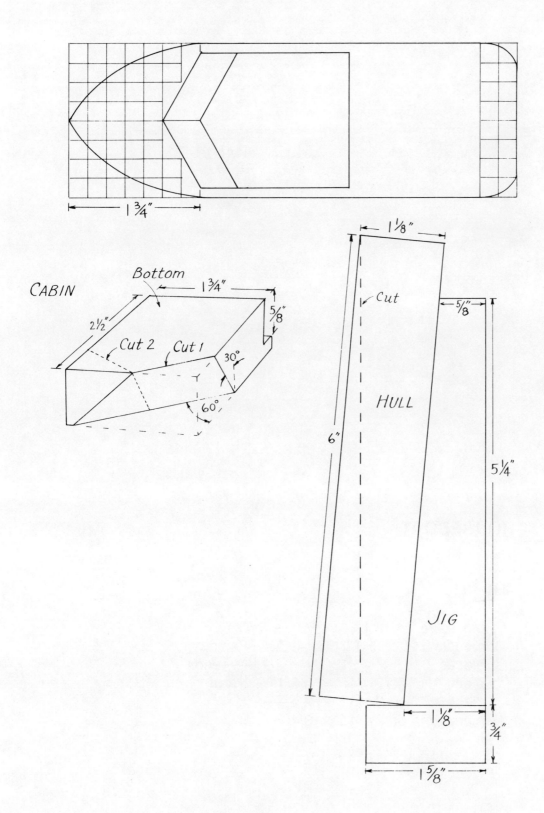

1 ¾"

CABIN

Bottom 1 ¾"

2 ½"

⅝"

Cut 2   Cut 1   30°

60°

1 ⅛"

Cut

⅝"

HULL

6"

5 ¼"

JIG

1 ⅛"

1 ⅛"

¾"

1 ⅝"

125

HOUSEBOAT

Materials

1 piece 3/4″ × 2 1/2″ × 7″——hull
2 pieces 1/4″ × 1 1/2″ × 4 1/2″——sides
2 pieces 7/16″ × 1 1/2″ × 1 1/2″——ends
1 piece 1/4″ × 2 1/4″ × 5 3/4″——roof
1 piece 1/4″ × 2 1/4″ × 2″——A
1 piece 1/4″ × 2 1/4″ × 3/4″——B

126

Construction

1. Shape the hull by sawing the back end (stern) with the saw tilted at 30 degrees. Saw along each side with the saw set at 15 degrees. Round off the front end or bow (see diagram).

2. Cut out 3/4″ × 3/4″ openings in the sides for the windows. The windows are 1″ from the ends. A good way to do this is to draw the windows on a piece of 3/4″ stock 4 1/2″ long. With the saw blade 3/4″ above the table make several passes through the piece. Then rip out the 1/4″ sides.

3. The front end window is also 3/4″ × 3/4″ while the doorway is 3/4″ × 1 1/4″.

4. Using a waterproof glue, fasten the sides to the ends. Round off one end (rear) of the roof and glue it to the ends and sides. It will extend 1 1/4″ in the back and 1/8″ on each side.

5. Round off the front end of the A piece and glue the B piece to it even with the back end. Saw this end at a 30-degree angle and glue the pieces to the roof even with the end.

6. Glue the assembled cabin to the hull equidistant from the ends and sides.

7. Finish the houseboat with a material recommended for boats.

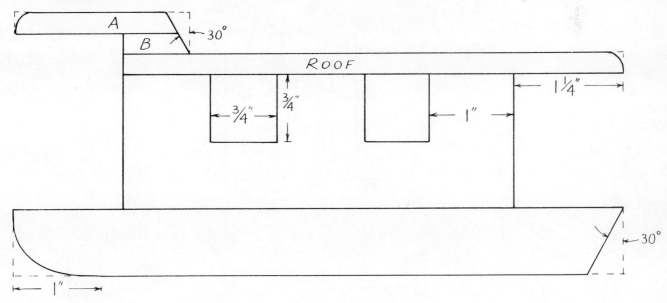

Pattern for PROW

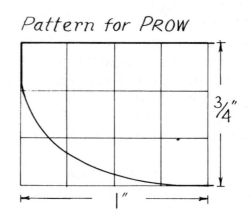

¾"

1"

Rear View

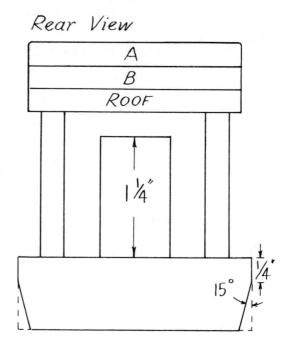

A

B

ROOF

1¼"

15°

¼"

PONTOON BOATS FOR WATER OR FLOOR

Materials

    2 pieces 1 1/8″ × 1 1/2″ × 10″——pontoons
    3 pieces 1/4″ dowel 2 1/4″ long——cross braces
    1 piece 7/16″ × 3″ × 6″——deck
    2 pieces 7/16″ × 3/4″ × 6″——sides
    2 pieces 7/16″ × 1 3/4″ × 3″——ends
    6 pieces 1/4″ dowel 2 1/2″ long——posts
    2 pieces 1/4″ × 1/2″ × 3 1/2″——crosspieces   } roof supports
    1 piece 1/4″ × 3 1/2″ × 7 1/2″——roof

129

Construction

    1. In the inside surface of each pontoon drill three 1/4″ holes 1/2″ deep and 1/2″ from the upper edge. Locate the holes 2″ from either end with one in the middle.

    2. Round off the front ends of the pontoons.

    3. Using a waterproof glue, fasten the cross braces in the holes.

    4. In the 7/16″ edge of each side piece drill three 1/4″ holes 1/2″ deep. Locate the holes 1 1/2″ from the ends with one in the middle.

    5. Glue the sides to the deck even with the edges. Glue the ends to the sides and deck.

    6. In each of the roof crosspieces drill a 1/4″ hole 7/16″ from each end and centered.

    7. Glue the pieces to the underside of the roof 2″ from each end with one in the center.

    8. Drive the posts into the holes in the sides. Insert the posts into the holes in the crosspieces.

    9. Center the assembled cabin on the pontoons and glue in place. If making a floor toy, the procedure is the same except as follows:

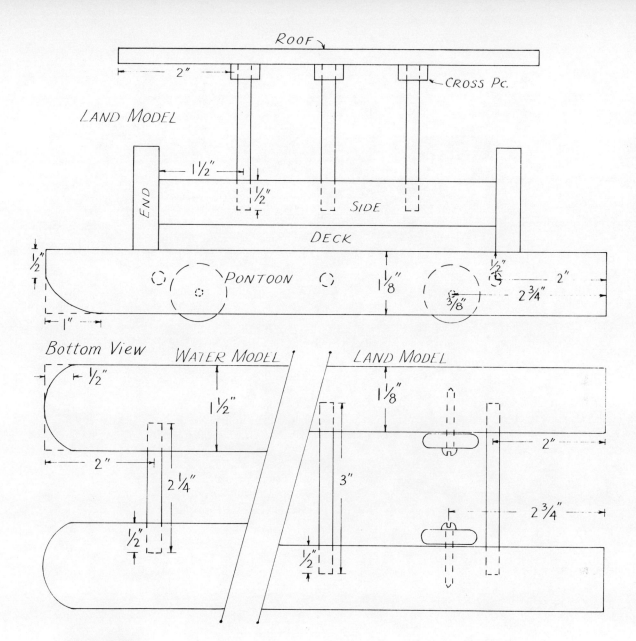

Materials

2 pieces 1 1/8″ × 1 1/8″ × 10″——pontoons
3 pieces 1/4″ dowel 3″ long——cross braces
4 no. 6——1″ roundhead screws
4   1″ wheels

Construction

1. In the inside surface of each pontoon drill pilot holes for the screws 2 3/4″ from the ends and 3/8″ from the lower edge.
2. Install the wheels before putting in the cross braces.

131

FREIGHTER

Materials

1 piece 1 1/8″ × 4″ × 14″ } hull
1 piece 3/4″ × 2 7/8″ × 14″ }
4 pieces 3/16″ dowel 1 1/4″ long——axles
4   1 1/4″ wheels about 3/8″ thick
1 piece 3/4″ × 1 3/4″ × 2″——x } superstructure
1 piece 7/16″ × 1 1/4″ × 1 1/2″——y }
1 piece 3/4″ dowel 1 1/2″ long——smokestack

Construction

This ship is a floor toy.

1. From the 1 1/8″ stock rip out lengthwise two pieces (A) 1/2″ thick; two pieces (B) 7/16″ thick; one piece (C) 1″ thick.

2. From the B pieces saw off four 2 1/2″ lengths and two 6″ lengths.

3. Glue the 2 1/2″ pieces to the A pieces even with the ends of A. Glue the 6″ pieces to A equidistant from the ends of A (see diagram).

4. Glue these assemblies to the middle or C piece.

5. Drill two 3/16″ holes in each side of the hull 3/8″ up from the bottom edge and 3 1/4″ from either end. Drill the holes through the wheel wells to a depth of 1 1/4″.

6. Glue the two sections of the hull together.

7. Shape the bow and stern using the diagrams as guides. A 10″ plate can be used when shaping the bow.

8. Along the 2″ sides of the x piece drill five 1/8″ holes about 1/4″ deep and evenly spaced. In the 1 1/2″ sides of the y piece drill three 1/8″ holes. Center the y piece on the x piece and glue it fast. In the center of the superstructure drill a 3/4″ hole 1/2″ deep for the smokestack. Glue this assembly to the hull about 7″ from the bow.

9. Drill holes in the wheels large enough so they will revolve on the 3/16″ axles. Set the wheels in the wells and insert the axles.

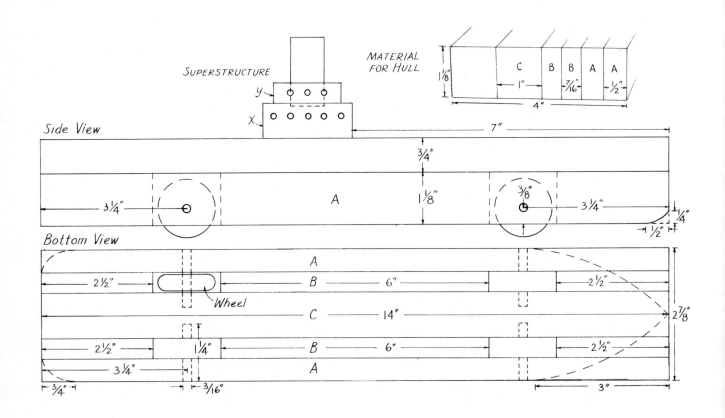

SUPERSTRUCTURE

MATERIAL FOR HULL

$1\frac{1}{8}$"

C B B A A

1" $\frac{7}{16}$" $\frac{1}{2}$"

4"

Side View

y

x

7"

$\frac{3}{4}$"

$3\frac{1}{4}$"

A

$1\frac{1}{8}$"

$\frac{3}{8}$"

$3\frac{1}{4}$"

$\frac{1}{4}$"

$\frac{1}{2}$"

Bottom View

$2\frac{1}{2}$"

A

B 6"

Wheel

$2\frac{1}{2}$"

C 14"

$2\frac{7}{8}$"

$2\frac{1}{2}$"

$1\frac{1}{4}$"

B 6"

$2\frac{1}{2}$"

$3\frac{1}{4}$"

A

$\frac{3}{4}$"

$\frac{3}{16}$"

3"

8
At the Airport

Terminal

Control Tower

Monoplane

Biplane

Twin-Engine Airplane

Helicopter

Jet

Tow Tractors and Trailers

Hangar

The three-level terminal building provides a focus for this set. You may wish to design a terminal along lines with which you are familiar to use with the air traffic control tower described here. If you prefer, the terminal shown can be built with just one or two levels.

The various aircraft have been designed to be as realistic in appearance as possible without being too difficult to construct. The tractors and trailers are used to haul passengers' baggage to and from the jet.

AIRPORT TERMINAL

Materials: Passenger Lounge

2 pieces 3/4″ × 5 1/2″ × 9″——sides
1 piece 3/4″ × 5 1/2″ × 10 1/2″——back
1 piece 3/4″ × 1 5/8″ × 10 1/2″——brace
2 pieces 7/16″ × 3/4″ × 5 1/2″——A
1 piece 1/4″ × 12″ × 12″——floor—plywood
1 piece 1/4″ × 12 1/2″ × 12″——roof—plywood
2 pieces 3/4″ × 3/4″ × 5 1/2″——roof supports
8 no. 6   1 1/2″ flathead screws
No. 16   1″ brads
4 pieces 3/4″ × 1″ × 8″——seats ⎫
3 pieces 1/4″ × 2″ × 8″——backs ⎭ benches

Construction: Passenger Lounge

1. In each side drill and countersink four holes for the screws (see diagram).

2. Screw the sides to the back. Install the brace even with the upper edges and front ends of the sides.

3. Glue the A pieces to the front ends of the sides.

4. Nail on the floor which will extend 2 1/2″ in front.

5. Nail on the roof which will extend 3″. Space the brads evenly along the sides and back and in 3/8″ from the edges.

6. Glue the roof supports to the floor and roof even with the front and side edges of the floor.

7. Assemble the benches.

PASSENGER LOUNGE

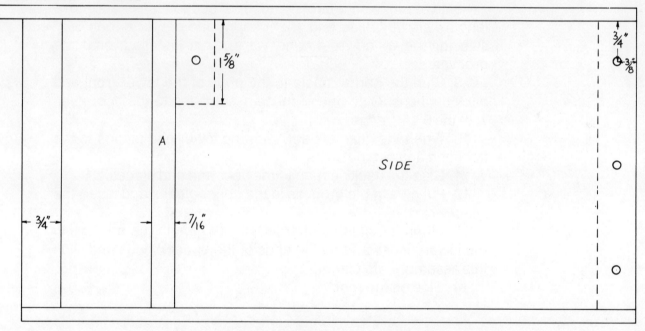

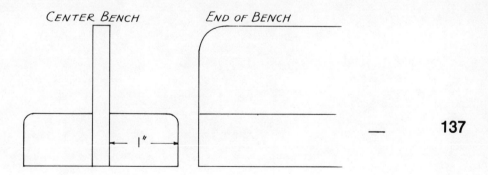

Materials: Office Section

2 pieces 3/4" × 2" × 8"——lower ⎫
2 pieces 3/4" × 1" × 8"——upper ⎬ front and back
2 pieces plastic 1/8" × 2" × 8" ⎭
2 pieces 3/4" × 2" × 6"——lower ⎫
2 pieces 3/4" × 1" × 6"——upper ⎬ ends
2 pieces plastic 1/8" × 2" × 6" ⎭
4 pieces 3/4" × 3/4" × 4"——corner posts
2 pieces 1/4" × 7 1/2" × 9 1/2"——floor and roof—
    plywood
No. 16   1" brads

Construction: Office Section

8. In each front, back, and end section saw a groove lengthwise 1/8" wide and 1/2" deep in the center of one 3/4" side for the windows. If windows are not installed, omit the grooves.

9. Glue the corner posts to the ends of the lower front and back sections. Glue one of these assemblies to the floor even with the 9 1/2" edge.

10. When the glue has set, glue the lower end pieces to the floor and against the posts.

11. Glue the back section to the floor and end pieces.

12. Put glue in the grooves in the upper pieces and insert the windows.

13. When the glue has hardened, put glue in the grooves in the lower pieces and on the ends of the upper pieces and slide this assembly into place.

14. Glue on the roof.

Materials: Traffic Control Room

2 pieces 3/4″ × 1″ × 3 1/2″——lower
2 pieces 3/4″ × 3/4″ × 3 1/2″——upper } front and back
2 pieces plastic 1/8″ × 2 1/2″ × 3 1/2″
2 pieces 3/4″ × 1″ × 2 1/2″——lower
2 pieces 3/4″ × 3/4″ × 2 1/2″——upper } ends
2 pieces plastic 1/8″ × 2 1/2″ × 2 1/2″
4 pieces 3/4″ × 3/4″ × 3 3/4″——corner posts
2 pieces 1/4″ × 4″ × 5″——floor and roof—plywood
1 piece 1/4″ × 2 7/16″ × 3 7/16″——roof underpiece

Construction: Control Room

15. Follow the same procedure in making the control room as the office section except that the grooves are 1/4″ deep instead of 1/2″.

16. Center the office section on the passenger lounge roof and glue in place.

17. Center the control room on the office section and glue in place.

18. Center the underpiece on the roof and glue in place.

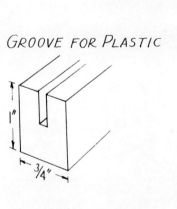

GROOVE FOR PLASTIC

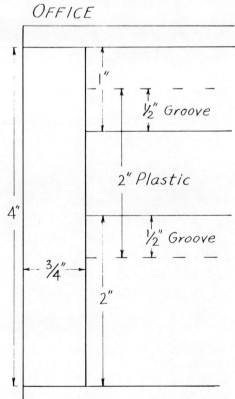

OFFICE

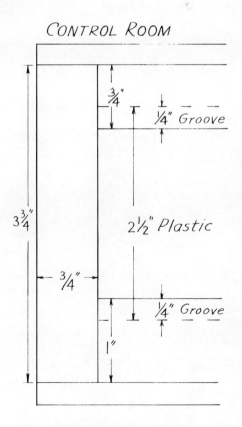

CONTROL ROOM

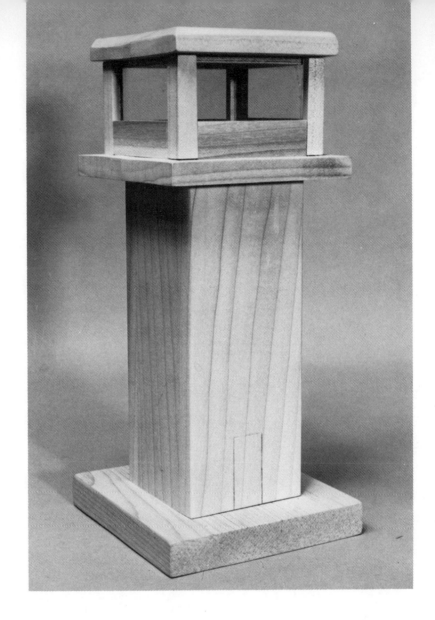

AIR TRAFFIC CONTROL TOWER

Materials

1 piece 3/4″ × 5″ × 5″——foundation
2 pieces 7/16″ × 2″ × 7″——ends ⎫
2 pieces 7/16″ × 3″ × 7″——sides ⎭ tower
1 piece 7/16″ × 4 1/2″ × 4 1/2″——floor
1 piece 7/16″ × 4″ × 4″——roof
1 piece 1/8″ × 2 11/16″ × 2 15/16″——roof underpiece
4 pieces 7/16″ × 7/16″ × 2″——corner posts
4 pieces plastic 1/8″ × 2″ × 3″——windows
2 pieces 3/16″ × 3/4″ × 2 1/2″——A
2 pieces 3/16″ × 3/4″ × 2 3/4″——B

Construction

1. In one side section, make grooves with an awl or sharp nail to represent a door. The door should be 3/4″ wide, 1 5/8″ high, and centered.

2. Glue the sides to the ends to make the tower.

3. Cut a rabbet in each corner post about 1/4″ × 1/4″. Glue the windows into the posts to make the control room.

4. Glue the room to the floor equidistant from the edges.

5. Glue the A and B pieces to the floor between the posts and against the outside of the windows.

6. With the saw tilted at 30 degrees saw off the upper edges of the roof. Center the underpiece on the roof and glue in place.

7. Glue the control room to the top of the tower, and the tower to the foundation.

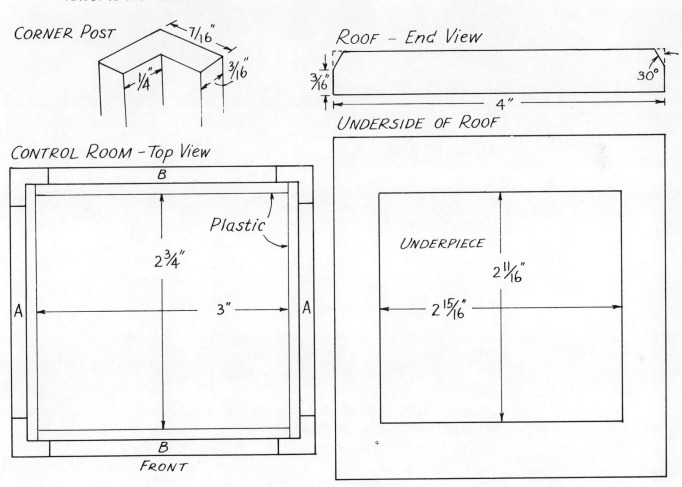

CORNER POST — 7/16″ — 1/4″ — 3/16″

ROOF – End View — 3/16″ — 4″ — 30°

UNDERSIDE OF ROOF

CONTROL ROOM – Top View

B — Plastic — 2 3/4″ — A — 3″ — A — B — FRONT

UNDERPIECE — 2 11/16″ — 2 15/16″

MONOPLANE

Materials

1 piece 1 1/8″ × 1 1/4″ × 7″——fuselage
1 piece 7/16″ × 1 1/8″ × 1 3/4″——cabin roof
1 piece 3/16″ × 1 1/4 × 10″——wing—plywood
1 piece 3/16″ × 3/4″ × 3″——stabilizer—plywood
1 piece 1/8″ × 1″ × 1 1/4″——rudder—plywood
1 piece 3/16″ × 1/4″ × 2″——propeller
2 pieces 3/16″ × 3/4″ × 3/4″——A ⎤
1 piece 1/4″ × 3/4″ × 2″——B   ⎬ landing gear
1 piece 3/16″ dowel 3″ long——axle ⎦
2   3/4″ wheels
1 piece 3/16″ dowel 3/4″ long——tail skid
1 no. 6   3/4″ roundhead screw
1 no. 6 machine screw washer

Construction

1. Shape the fuselage as shown in the diagrams. In the underside of the fuselage drill a 3/16" hole at an angle about 3/8" deep, 3/4" from the tail, and centered, for the tail skid (see diagram). Also, in the center of the nose drill a pilot hole for the propeller screw.

2. Round off all edges of the fuselage.

3. Round off the corners of the wing. In one side (front) cut an opening 1/8" deep and 1 1/8" long and equidistant from the ends (see diagram).

4. Set the saw at 30 degrees and saw off the front and rear ends of the cabin roof. Round off the top front edge. In each side of the roof drill two 1/4" holes about 1/4" in depth and 3/4" apart.

5. Glue the cabin roof to the fuselage 1" back from the nose. Glue the wing to the roof with the opening to the front to give the pilot better visibility.

6. In the center of the stabilizer make a saw cut across the grain 1/8" × 1/8". Round off the corners. Glue the rudder in the groove. Glue the assembly to the fuselage even with the end of the tail.

7. Shape the A pieces for the landing gear (see diagram). In each drill a 7/32" hole 3/16" from one edge (lower) and centered. Glue these pieces to the ends of the B piece.

8. Glue the landing gear assembly to the fuselage centered beneath the cabin.

9. Drill a hole for the screw in the center of the 1/4" side of the propeller.

10. Shape the propeller by shaving off the two front diagonally opposite corners (see diagram). Screw the propeller to the nose with the washer against the nose.

11. Drive in the tail skid and mount the wheels.

143

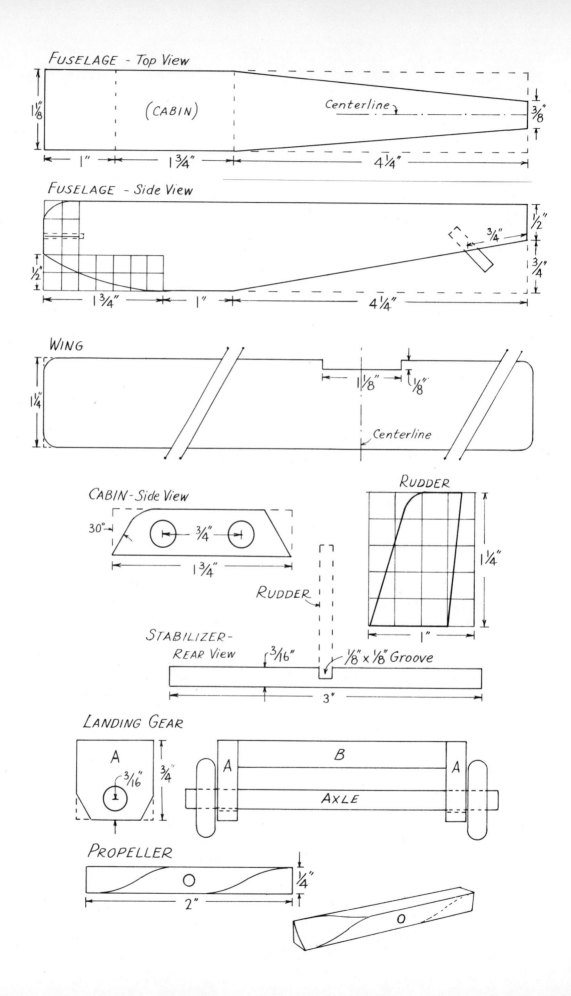

FUSELAGE - Top View

(CABIN)

Centerline

1⅛"

3⁄8"

1" 1¾" 4¼"

FUSELAGE - Side View

½"

¾"

½" ¾"

1¾" 1" 4¼"

WING

1¼"

1⅛" ⅛"

Centerline

CABIN - Side View

30° ¾"

1¾"

RUDDER

1¼"

1"

RUDDER

STABILIZER - REAR View

3⁄16" ⅛" x ⅛" Groove

3"

LANDING GEAR

A

3⁄16"

¾"

A B A

AXLE

PROPELLER

O

¼"

2"

O

144

BIPLANE

Materials

1 piece 1 1/8″ × 1 1/4″ × 7″——fuselage
1 piece 7/16″ × 1 1/8″ × 1 7/8″——cabin roof
2 pieces 3/16″ × 1 1/4″ × 10″——wings—plywood
1 piece 3/16″ × 3/4″ × 3″——stabilizer—plywood
1 piece 1/8″ × 1″ × 1 1/4″——rudder—plywood
1 piece 3/16″ × 1/4″ × 2″——propeller
4 pieces 3/16″ dowel about 1 1/2″ long——struts
4 pieces 3/16″ × 3/8″ × 1 1/4″——x
2 pieces 3/16″ × 3/4″ × 3/4″——A ⎫
1 piece 1/4″ × 3/4″ × 2″——B ⎬ landing gear
1 piece 3/16″ dowel 3″ long——axle ⎪
2　　3/4″ wheels ⎭
1 piece 3/16″ dowel 3/4″ long——tail skid
1 no. 6　　3/4″ roundhead screw
1 no. 6　　machine screw washer

Construction

1. Shape the fuselage as shown in the diagram. In the underside drill a 3/16″ hole at an angle 3/8″ deep, 3/4″ from the end of the tail, and centered, for the tail skid (see diagram). Drill a pilot hole for the screw in the center of the nose.

2. Round off all edges of the fuselage and the corners of the wings.

3. Drill two 3/16″ holes in each x piece 1/4″ from the ends and centered. Glue these pieces to the wings 1 1/4″ from the ends.

4. With the saw blade tilted at 30 degrees saw off the front and rear ends of the cabin roof. Round off the front top edge. Drill two 1/4″ holes in each side of the cabin roof 1/4″ deep and 3/4″ apart.

5. Glue the roof to the fuselage about 1″ from the nose.

6. In the center of the stabilizer make a saw cut across the grain 1/8″ × 1/8″. Round off the corners. Shape the rudder (see diagram), and glue it in the saw cut.

7. Shape the A pieces (see diagram). Drill a 7/32″ hole in each, 3/16″ from the lower edge and centered. Glue the A pieces to the ends of B.

8. Glue the lower wing in the opening made in the fuselage. Put glue in the holes in the x pieces on the lower wing and insert the struts. Attach the upper wing in the same way.

9. Glue the landing gear to the wing equidistant from the ends and centered. Mount the wheels.

10. Drill a hole for the screw in the 1/4″ side of the propeller.

11. Shape the propeller by shaving off the two front diagonally opposite corners (see diagram). Fasten the propeller to the nose with the washer against the nose.

12. Insert the tail skid and glue the stabilizer assembly to the fuselage even with the end of the tail.

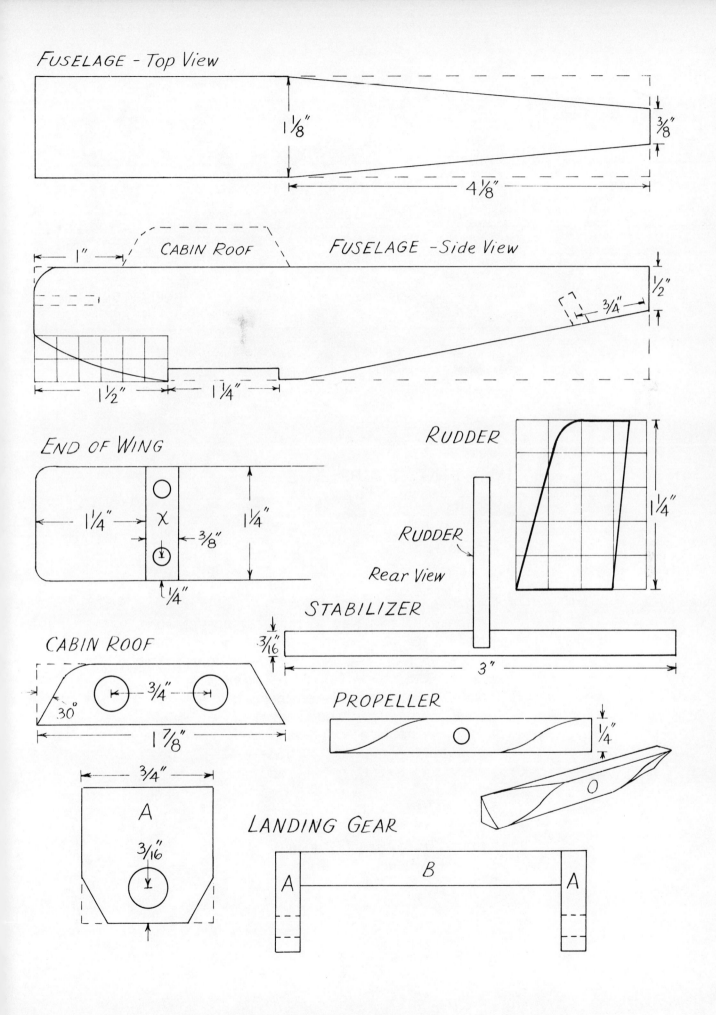

FUSELAGE - Top View

1⅛"

⅜"

4⅛"

CABIN ROOF   FUSELAGE - Side View

1"

½"

¾"

1½"   1¼"

END OF WING

1¼"

X

⅜"

1¼"

¼"

RUDDER

1¼"

RUDDER

Rear View

STABILIZER

3/16"

3"

CABIN ROOF

30°

¾"

1⅞"

PROPELLER

¼"

O

LANDING GEAR

¾"

A

3/16"

A   B   A

TWIN-ENGINE AIRPLANE

Materials

1 piece 1 1/2″ × 1 1/2″ × 9″
       or   } fuselage
2 pieces 3/4″ × 1 1/2″ × 9″
1 piece 3/4″ × 1 1/2″ × 2 1/2″——cabin roof
1 piece 3/16″ × 1 1/2″ × 12″——wing—plywood
1 piece 3/16″ × 1″ × 3″——stabilizer—plywood
1 piece 1/8″ × 1 1/4″ × 1 1/2″——rudder—plywood
2 pieces 3/16″ × 1/4″ × 2″——propellers
2 wooden clothespins——engines
2 no. 6   3/4″ roundhead screws
2 no. 6   machine screw washers
4 pieces 3/16″ × 3/4″ × 1 1/8″——A—plywood }
1 piece 1/4″ × 3/4″ × 3″——B
1 piece 1/4″ × 1/2″ × 3/4″——C
3 pieces 7/16″ × 1/2″ × 3/4″——D   } landing gear
1 piece 3/16″ dowel 4″ long——axle
1 piece 3/16″ dowel 7/8″ long
3   3/4″ wheels

Construction

1. Shape the fuselage as shown in the diagrams and round off all edges. If using the two 3/4″ pieces, glue them together to make a piece 1 1/2″ × 1 1/2″.

2. In the underside of the fuselage make an opening 3/16″ × 1 1/2″ for the wing (see diagram).

3. Round off the corners of the wing.

4. With the saw set at 30 degrees saw off the front and back ends of the cabin roof. Then shape the roof as shown rounding off all edges. Drill three 1/4″ holes in each side 5/8″ apart, about 1/4″ deep, and up 1/4″ from the lower edge.

5. In the center of the stabilizer saw a 1/8″ × 1/8″ groove across the grain. Round off the corners. Shape the rudder and glue it in this groove.

6. In the center of each propeller drill a hole for the screw on which it will revolve.

7. With a file enlarge the openings in the clothespins so they will fit on the wing. Saw off the ends so they are even with the back edge of the wing.

8. Shape the propellers by shaving off the two front diagonally opposite corners (see diagram). Fasten them to the clothespins with the washer against the head.

9. To make the landing gear shape the A pieces (see diagram). Drill a 7/32″ hole in each 3/16″ from the lower edge and centered.

10. Glue an A piece to each end of the B piece. Also glue an A piece to each 1/2″ side of the C piece. To strengthen the landing gear, glue a D piece to the B piece and against each A piece.

11. Drill two or more holes about 1 1/4″ deep in the underside of the nose for pieces of metal about 1″ long which will balance the airplane. Otherwise, it will fall back on the tail when the landing gear is attached. Two 3/8″ holes into which 1″ pieces of 3/8″ rod are put should do. Plug the holes with pieces of 3/8″ dowel. Some experimentation may be necessary to get the desired result. The landing gear can be held in place with rubber bands while doing this.

12. Glue the wing in the opening made in the fuselage.

13. Install the wheels and fasten the two-wheel assembly to the wing equidistant from the ends.

14. Glue the single wheel assembly to the fuselage about 1/2″ back from the nose. Glue the remaining D piece to the fuselage and against this assembly.

15. Fasten the engines to the wing about 3 3/4″ from either end.

16. Glue on the cabin roof about 2″ back from the nose. Glue the stabilizer assembly to the fuselage even with the end of the tail.

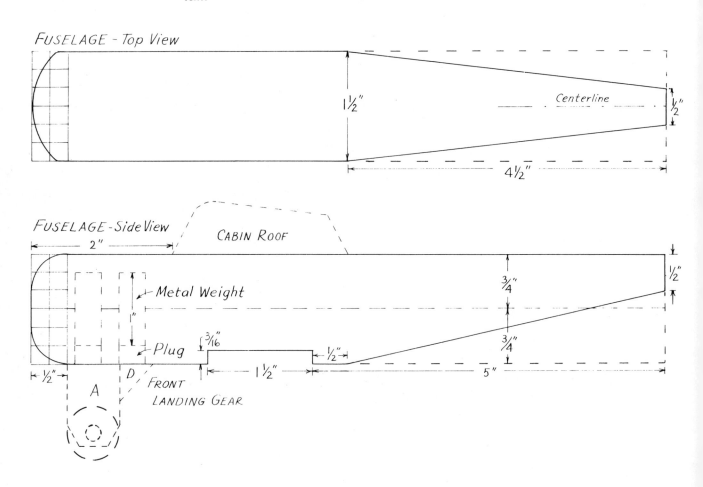

150

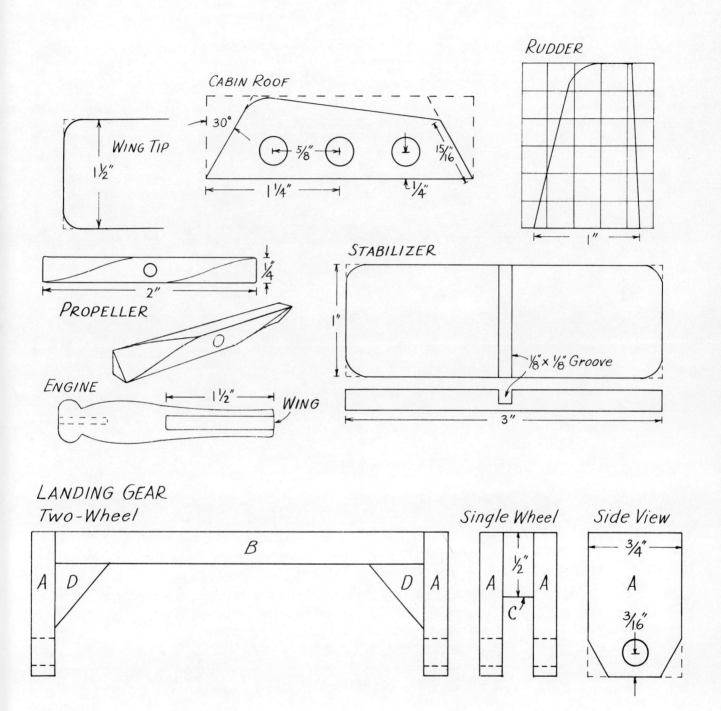

RUDDER

CABIN ROOF

30°   5/8"   15/16"

1 1/4"   1/4"

WING TIP

1 1/2"

PROPELLER

2"   1/4"

STABILIZER

1"

1/8" x 1/8" Groove

3"

ENGINE

1 1/2"   WING

LANDING GEAR
Two-Wheel

B

A D   D A

Single Wheel

A   A
1/2"
C

Side View

3/4"

A

3/16"

151

HELICOPTER

Materials

1 piece 1 1/2″ × 2″ × 9″——fuselage
1 piece 7/16″ × 2″ × 3″——engine compartment
1 piece 3/16″ × 1/2″ × 7 1/2″——main rotor
1 piece 3/16″ × 1/4″ × 2″——tail rotor
1 piece 1/8″ × 1/2″ × 3″——stabilizer ⎫
1 piece 1/8″ × 3/4″ × 2 1/2″——rudder ⎬ tail assembly
1 piece 7/16″ × 1″ × 2 1/2″——A
2 pieces 7/16″ × 3/8″ × 4 1/2″——runners
2 pieces 1/4″ × 1/2″ × 4 1/2″——braces
1 bead 1/2″ to 3/4″ long
1 no. 6   1 1/4″ roundhead screw
1 no. 6   3/4″ roundhead screw
2 no. 6 machine screw washers

Construction

1. In one side (upper) of the fuselage cut an opening 1/2" wide, 1/8" deep, and 1 3/4" from the tail for the stabilizer.

2. Shape the fuselage as shown in the diagrams. Round off all edges.

3. In each side of the cabin drill four 5/16" holes 1/4" deep and 3/4" apart. Locate the first hole 1 3/4" back from the nose and 1/4" from the upper surface.

4. Round off the ends of the roof and engine compartment. Glue it to the fuselage about 1 3/8" from the nose.

5. In the top center of the engine compartment drill a pilot hole for the 1 1/4" screw. Also drill a pilot hole in the left side of the tail 1/2" from the end for the screw for the tail rotor.

6. Shape the rudder (see diagram).

7. Round off one end of the runners. Cut 1/4" × 1/2" grooves in each 1 1/8" from either end.

8. Glue the braces in the grooves in the runners.

9. Glue the landing skid to the A piece.

10. Glue the landing assembly to the fuselage 1 1/4" from the nose and centered.

11. Drill a hole for a screw through the center of each rotor.

12. Shape the rotors by cutting off two diagonally opposite edges of the top surface (see diagram).

13. Install the rotors.

14. Glue the stabilizer in the groove in the fuselage.

15. Glue the rudder to the side of the fuselage opposite the tail rotor.

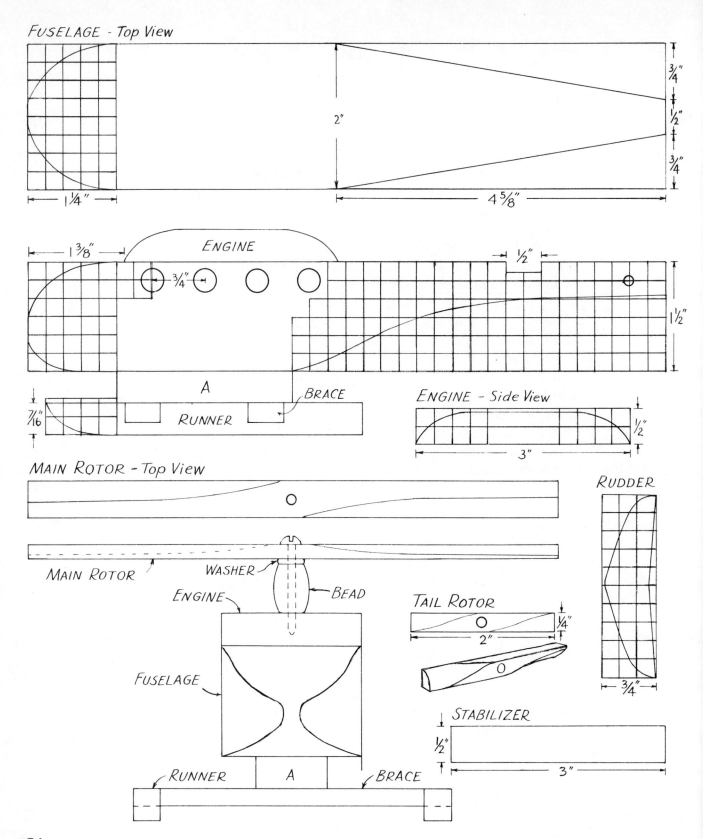

FUSELAGE - Top View

2"

3/4"

1/2"

3/4"

1 1/4"

4 5/8"

1 3/8"

ENGINE

3/4"

1/2"

1 1/2"

7/16"

A

RUNNER

BRACE

ENGINE - Side View

3"

1/2"

MAIN ROTOR - Top View

MAIN ROTOR

WASHER

BEAD

ENGINE

FUSELAGE

RUNNER   A   BRACE

TAIL ROTOR

1/4"

2"

RUDDER

3/4"

STABILIZER

1/2"

3"

154

JET AIRPLANE

Materials

1 piece 1 1/8″ × 1 3/8″ × 13 1/2″——lower
    section } fuselage
1 piece 7/16″ × 1 3/8″ × 12 1/2″——upper
    section
1 piece 3/16″ × 2 1/4″ × 13 1/4″——wing
1 piece 3/16″ × 1 1/2″ × 5″——stabilizer
1 piece 1/8″ × 2 1/4″ × 2″——rudder
4 wooden clothespins——engines
3 pieces 7/16″ × 1/2″ × 1″——axle holders }
3 pieces 3/16″ × 1″ × 1″——A } landing gear
3 pieces 3/16″ dowel 1″ long——axles
6   3/4″ wheels

Construction

1. Set the saw at 30 degrees and saw off one end (front) of the upper fuselage section.

2. Make the stabilizer (see diagram). In the center of the stabilizer cut a groove, across the grain, 1/8″ wide and about 3/32″ deep for the rudder.

155

3. Using the same saw setting for depth, cut an opening in the upper side of the top section 1 1/2" wide and 1/2" in from the end of the tail.

4. Shape the rudder and glue it in the groove made in the stabilizer.

5. In the underside of the lower section of the fuselage make an opening for the wing 3/16" deep, 2 1/4" long, and 4 1/2" back from the nose. Shape the nose (see diagram).

6. Shape the wing (see diagram).

7. Saw off one prong of each clothespin and drill a 1/4" hole about 1/4" deep in the head of each. Saw off the ends of the remaining prong of two clothespins so that the pins are 3" long. Make the other two 2 5/8" long. File the back end of the body of each pin at an angle to conform to the angle of the wing (see diagram).

8. Glue the 3" clothespins to the underside of the wing so that each will be about 1" from the fuselage when the wing is attached.

9. Glue the other two clothespins to the wing 1 1/8" from the first ones. They should be parallel to the fuselage when the wing is in place.

10. Drill a 7/32" hole 3/16" from the end (lower) of each axle holder. Round off this end.

11. Glue the axle holders to the center of the A pieces.

12. Drill a 3/16" hole down through the center of the A pieces into the axle holders to a depth of about 5/8". Put glue into the holes and drive in pieces of 3/16" dowel.

13. Install the wheels. Glue a wheel assembly to the wing between the engines and even with the back edge of the wing.

14. Along each side of the lower section of the fuselage drill sixteen 1/8" holes about 1/4" deep and 1/2" apart for the windows. Locate the first hole 3" from the nose and 3/16" from the upper surface.

15. At this point steps must be taken to balance the airplane or it will fall back on the tail when the landing gear is in place. This can be partially accomplished by drilling several 1/2" or 3/4" holes about 7/8" deep in the center of the lower section of the fuselage. Start the first hole about 2" from the tail and drill holes for 6" or so to the center of the opening for the wing. This will lighten the fuselage behind the wing.

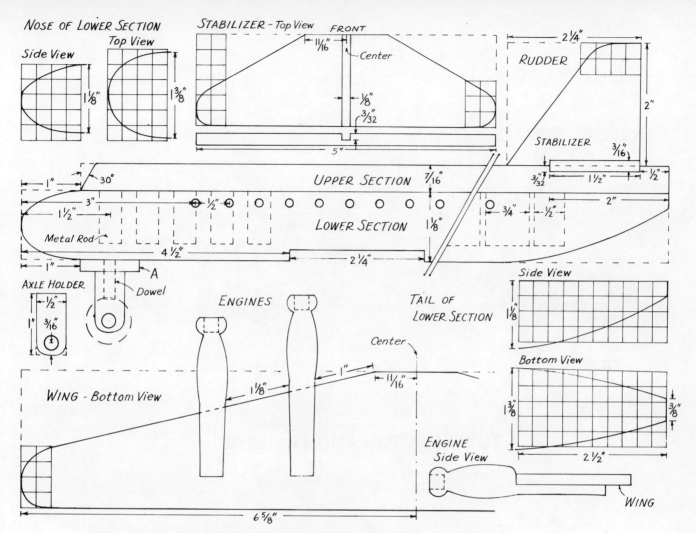

16. It will also be necessary to add weight to the fuselage in front of the wing. Drill four or five 3/8″ holes about 7/8″ deep and insert pieces of 3/8″ rod. Locate the first hole 1 1/2″ back from the nose. Some experimentation will be necessary to obtain the desired result. The wing assembly and front landing gear can be attached to the fuselage with rubber bands while working for the correct balance. If, after the jet is entirely assembled, any problem should arise a hole or two can be drilled in the underside of the fuselage 1″ or so from the nose. Pieces of rod can be put into these holes and the holes plugged with pieces of dowel.

17. Glue the upper section to the lower section 1″ from the nose.

18. Shape the tail (see diagram).

19. Round off all edges of the fuselage.

20. Glue the wing and stabilizer assemblies in place.

21. Glue the front landing gear to the fuselage about 1″ from the nose.

TOW TRACTOR AND TRAILERS

Materials

```
1 piece 7/16″ × 2 1/4″ × 4 1/4″        ⎫
              or                        ⎬ frame
1 piece 7/16″ × 1 3/4″ × 4 1/4″——A     ⎪
2 pieces 1/4″ × 7/16″ × 1 3/4″——B      ⎭
1 piece 1 1/8″ × 2 1/4″ × 1 3/4″——engine
1 piece 7/16″ × 2 1/4″ × 1 1/2″——back section
1 piece 7/16″ × 3/4″ × 5/8″——bottom    ⎫
1 piece 1/4″ × 3/4″ × 1″——back          ⎬ seat
1 piece 3/16″ dowel 1 3/4″ long——steering shaft
1     1″ wheel——steering wheel
1 piece 3/16″ × 1/2″ × 5 1/4″          ⎫
1 piece 3/16″ × 1/2″ × 1″——C            ⎬ coupler bar
1 piece 7/16″ × 1″ × 1 3/4″——rear axle holder
1 piece 7/16″ × 3/4″ × 1 3/4″——front axle holder
1 piece 1/4″ dowel 2 3/4″ long——rear axle
1 piece 3/16″ dowel 2 3/8″ long——front axle
2     1 1/4″ wheels——rear
2     1″ wheels——front
2 small furniture nails——headlights
```

158

Construction

1. In the center of the bottom of the frame saw a groove lengthwise 3/16″ deep and 1/2″ wide for the coupler bar.

2. Glue the C piece to one end of the coupler bar. Drill a 9/32″ hole 3/8″ from this end and centered. Round off the end. Glue the bar in the groove. It should be even with or slightly below the surface of the frame.

3. Shape the frame as shown in the diagram, or if using the A and B pieces, glue the B pieces to the side edges of the A piece 1 1/4″ from the ends. The end result will be the same.

4. In the center of the top surface of the rear axle holder saw a groove lengthwise about 9/32″ × 9/32″ so that the 1/4″ dowel axle will turn easily in it. Glue the holder to the frame even with the rear end.

5. In the front axle holder drill a 7/32″ hole lengthwise through the center. Glue the holder to the frame 1/4″ back from the front end.

6. Tilt the saw blade at 30 degrees and saw off the upper front end of the engine. With the saw set at 15 degrees saw along the side edges (see diagram).

7. In the back end of the engine drill a 13/64″ hole at an angle downward about 1″ deep and 3/4″ from the left side for the steering shaft.

8. Drive in the headlights about 1/2″ up from the lower edge and 1/4″ from the side edges.

9. Glue the engine to the frame even with the end.

10. Shape the front and back ends of the rear section with the saw set at 15 degrees. Saw a 1/8″ by 1/4″ wide piece out of each side to provide clearance for the wheels (see diagram). Glue the section to the frame even with the end.

11. Assemble and install the steering wheel and seat.

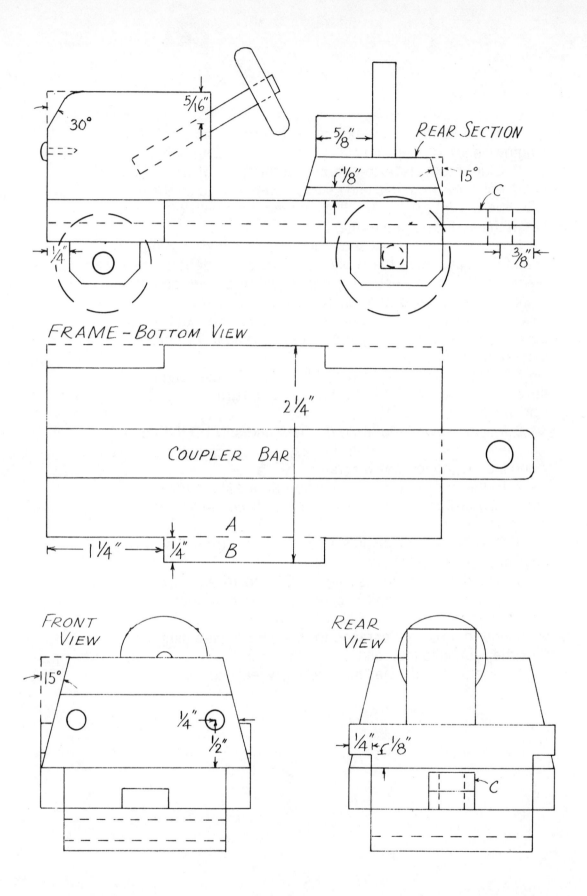

5/16"

30°

REAR SECTION

5/8"

1/8"

15°

C

1/4"

3/8"

FRAME–BOTTOM VIEW

2 1/4"

COUPLER BAR

A

B

1 1/4"

1/4"

FRONT VIEW

15°

1/4"

1/2"

REAR VIEW

1/4"

1/8"

C

160

FOUR TRAILERS FOR THE TOW TRACTOR

Materials: Trailer No. 1

1 piece 7/16″ × 2″ × 5″——deck
1 piece 3/16″ × 1/2″ × 7 1/2″——bar ⎫
1 piece 1/4″ dowel 7/8″ long (or use axle pin)—— ⎬ coupler
    hitch ⎭
4 pieces 7/16″ × 7/8″ × 1″ ⎫
2 pieces 7/16″ × 1″ × 5/8″——A ⎬ axle holders
2 pieces 3/16″ dowel 2 1/8″ long——axles
4   1″ wheels

The materials for the other trailers are, for the most part, the same as those for the first trailer. Any additional materials needed are listed.

Trailer No. 2

2 pieces 7/16″ × 1 1/4″ × 2″——ends

Trailer No. 3

2 pieces 7/16″ × 1 5/8″ × 2″——ends
1 piece 1/4″ × 2″ × 5″——roof
1 piece 1/8″ × 2″ × 4 1/2″——shelf

Trailer No. 4

2 pieces 7/16″ × 1 5/8″ × 2″——ends
1 piece 1/4″ × 2 1/8″ × 5″——roof
1 piece 1/8″ × 2″ × 4 1/2″——shelf
1 piece 1/8″ × 2″ × 2 1/16″——back

161

TRAILER 3

Construction: Trailer No. 1

1. In the center of the deck saw a groove lengthwise 3/16″ deep and 1/2″ wide for the coupler bar.

2. In one end of the bar drill a 9/32″ hole and in the other end drill a 1/4″ hole. The holes should be 3/8″ from the ends and centered. Round off the ends.

3. Glue the bar in the groove letting it extend 1 1/2″ at one end (front) or where the 1/4″ hole is. The bar should be in the underside of the deck of the first trailer.

4. When more than one trailer is being made, the bar in the second one should be in the upper side of the deck. If a third trailer is made, the bar should be in the underside and the dowel hitch should extend upward.

5. With the miter gauge at 60 degrees shape the axle holders. Drill a 7/32″ hole through each holder 1/4″ from the lower edge. Glue a holder to each end of the A piece (see diagram).

6. Glue the axle holder assemblies to the underside of the deck 1/2″ from either end and 1/4″ from the side edges.

7. Put the hitch in the coupler bar. It should extend downward. A small hole may be drilled through one side edge of the bar into the hitch and a piece of round toothpick or applicator stick inserted.

The steps for the construction of the other trailers are the same up to this point. Additional directions are as follows:

Trailer No. 2

Round off two corners (upper) of the ends and glue them to the deck.

Trailer No. 3

1. In the center of each end piece saw a groove 1/8″ wide and 3/16″ deep for the shelf. The shelf may be left out to make more room or it may be removable.

2. Glue on the roof.

Trailer No. 4

Follow the directions for No. 3. Glue the back on before the roof.

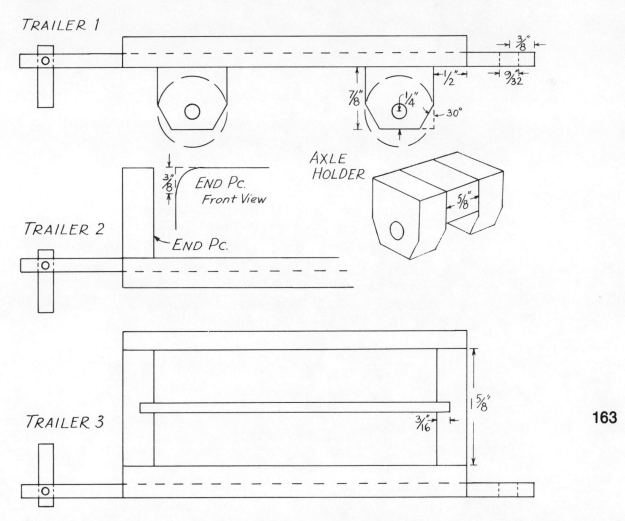

TRAILER 1

TRAILER 2

TRAILER 3

END PC.
Front View

END PC.

AXLE HOLDER

163

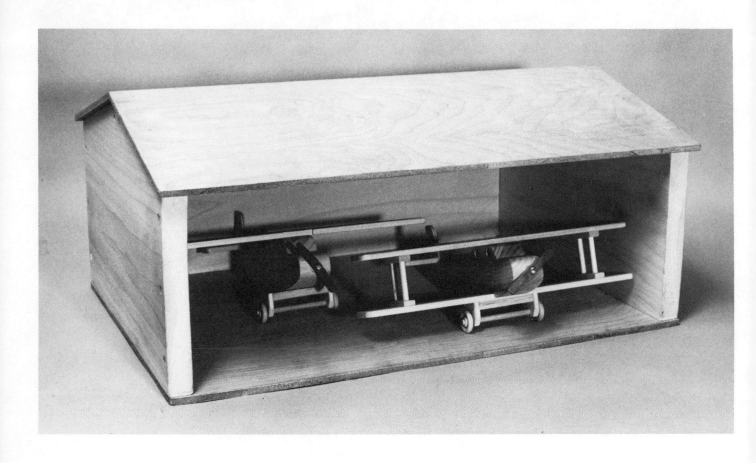

HANGAR

Materials

2 pieces 3/4″ × 7 1/2″ × 12″——ends
1 piece 3/4″ × 7 1/2″ × 16″——back
2 pieces 1/4″ × 6 3/4″ × 18″——roof—plywood
1 piece 1/4″ × 12″ × 17 1/2″——floor—plywood
2 pieces 3/4″ × 1 1/8″ × 16″——ridge brace
10 no. 6   1 1/2″ flathead screws
No. 16   1″ and 3/4″ brads

Construction

1. Across one edge (upper) of one end piece draw a line at the midpoint or 6″ from either end. Set the miter gauge at 75 degrees. With the end of the piece against the wood facing, fastened to the miter gauge, saw from this line to the edge thus removing the corner. Turn the piece over and repeat the operation. If a stop is fastened with a C clamp to the facing and against the back edge of the piece it will prevent creeping.

2. In each end piece drill and countersink five holes for the screws. The three holes along the back should be in 3/8″ from the edge and 1″, 3″, and 5″ from the lower edge. Locate the holes for the ridge brace by measuring 1/2″ down from the peak on the center line and 3/8″ to either side of the line.

3. Saw a strip off the back so that the remaining piece is 5 7/8″ wide. Set the saw at 15 degrees and saw off one top side edge of the back so that it will conform to the slant of the roof.

4. With the saw blade tilted at 15 degrees cut a narrow strip lengthwise off one edge of each roof board. Be sure that the side , which will be the underside, is facing upward. When the two pieces are joined at the peak, they will form the same angle as the ends.

5. With the 15-degree setting saw off one 3/4″ side of each ridge brace piece. When the 1 1/8″ sides are glued together, they will form the same angle as the ends.

6. Screw the ends to the back. Set the ridge brace in place and drive in the screws.

7. Nail on the floor.

8. Drill five pilot holes 5/8″ in from the ends of the roof boards and 1 1/4″ apart for the brads. Locate the first hole 1 1/4″ from the lower edges.

9. Nail one roof board on. It will extend 1/4″ at each end. Set the other board in place against the first so as to form a tight joint at the peak and nail it fast. Three 3/4″ brads along each side of the peak spaced 4 1/2″ apart and 1/2″ from the peak should do.

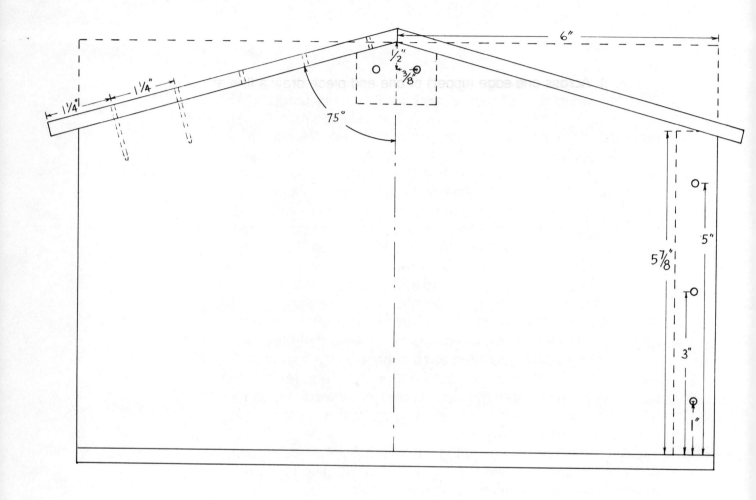

9
Larger Toys to Make

Pumper
Ladder Truck
Fire Chief's Station Wagon
Police Car
Racer

The toys here are for the toymaker who wishes to try his hand at making larger and more detailed toys. As with all the toys in this book, the designs are simplified in comparison with the real item, but every effort has been made to make the finished appearance and proportions realistic.

PUMPER

Materials

1 piece 7/16″ × 4″ × 13 3/4″
1 piece 7/16″ × 3/8″ × 4″——end piece } frame

1 piece 3/4″ × 1 1/2″ × 3″——front
1 piece 3/4″ × 1 1/2″ × 2″——rear } axle holders

2 pieces 1 1/8″ × 4″ × 4 1/2″
1 piece 3/4″ × 4″ × 4 1/2″ } cab

1 piece 7/16″ × 3/4″ × 4 1/8″——bumper—hardwood

1 piece 1 1/8″ × 1 1/2″ × 1 1/2″——x
1 piece 3/4″ × 1 1/2″ × 1 1/2″——y } Z

2 pieces 7/16″ × 2 1/4″ × 2 1/4″——ends
2 pieces 7/16″ × 2 1/4″ × 3 1/16″——sides
1 piece 1/4″ × 2 1/4″ × 3 15/16″——top } pump panel section
2 pieces 3/8″ dowel 1/2″ long——hose connectors
4 pieces 3/16″ dowel 1/2″ long——hose connectors

2 pieces 7/16″ × 3/4″ × 1 1/16″——ends
2 pieces 7/16″ × 3/4″ × 3 1/4″——sides
2 pieces 3/4″ dowel 1″ long——reels } reel rack
2 pieces 3/16″ dowel 1 3/4″ long——axles

168

```
2 pieces 7/16″ × 2″ × 1 5/8″——ends  ⎫
2 pieces 7/16″ × 2″ × 4 3/4″——sides  ⎬ tank
1 piece 1/4″ × 2 1/2″ × 4 3/4″——top  ⎭
2 pieces 1/4″ × 1 3/4″ × 4 3/4″——A
2 pieces 3/4″ × 1 1/8″ × 5″——fenders
2 pieces 7/16″ × 3/4″ × 4 3/4″——ladder holders—
    hardwood
4 pieces 1/4″ × 1/4″ × 4 7/8″——rails—  ⎫
    hardwood                            ⎬ ladders
36 pieces 1/8″ dowel 5/8″ long——rungs  ⎭
8 no. 6    1″ round-or pan-head screws
4 furniture nails——headlights
1 piece 1/2″ dowel 1″ long (or use axle pin)——
    warning light
2 pieces 1/4″ dowel 4 1/4″ long——axles
6    2″ wheels
```

Construction

1. In the frame cut out openings for the wheel wells. The front wells are 1 1/2″ from the end, 1/2″ deep, and 2 3/16″ wide. The rear wells are 2 3/16″ from the end, 1″ deep, and 2 3/16″ wide. In the underside of the frame drill 8 holes for the screws (see diagram).

2. Shape the axle holders (see page 7). Cut a 9/32″ × 9/32″ groove lengthwise in the center of each. Glue the holders to the frame so that the center of the groove is in the center of the wheel well.

3. Glue the end piece to the back end of the frame.

4. Set the saw at 15 degrees and saw off the front and back ends of one of the 1 1/8″ pieces for the cab. Glue the three pieces together with the 3/4″ piece in the middle. Drill a hole in the top 1″ from the front edge and centered for the warning light. With a 2 1/2″ Forsner or Greenlee type bit cut an arc 1 1/2″ from the front end and 1/2″ deep in each side of the cab for the front fender. The top edge of the arc should be up 5/8″ from the lower edge of the cab.

5. Drive in the headlights 3/8″ and 7/8″ from the side edges and 1 1/2″ from the lower edge. Glue on the bumper and glue the cab to the frame even with the front end.

6. Make the Z piece by gluing x to y. Center Z on the frame and glue it to the frame and against the cab.

7. Make the pump panel section by gluing the sides to the ends. Glue on the top. Drill a 3/8" hole in each end 1/4" deep, 3/4" from the lower edge, and centered. Drill two 3/16" holes 1 1/4" from the lower edge, 1/2" from the side edges, and 1/4" deep. Glue the hose connectors in these holes. Glue the pump section to the base and against the Z piece.

8. In one side of the reel rack drill a 7/32" hole 1" from either end and 1/4" from one side edge (upper). In the other side drill corresponding 3/16" holes, but only 1/4" deep. Through the center of each reel drill a 7/32" hole. Assemble the rack, making sure that the holes are opposite each other. Put glue in the 3/16" holes and install the reels. Center the rack on the top of the pump section and glue in place.

9. Place each fender piece over the wheel wells with the front end against the pump section. Mark the location of the arc. With the Forstner or Greenlee type bit cut an opening in each fender. The top of the arc should be 5/8" from the lower edge.

10. Glue the sides of the tank to the ends and glue on the top.

11. Place the fenders against the tank and mark the location of the arc on each side of the tank. Cut an arc about 1/4" deep to provide clearance for the inner wheels.

12. Glue the tank to the frame and the fenders to the frame and against the tank.

13. Round off the top corners of the A pieces. Glue them to the fenders and against the tank.

14. Cut a rabbet in each ladder holder 1/2" deep and 9/32" wide (see diagram). Glue a holder to each fender and against the A pieces.

15. To make the rails for the ladders, draw parallel lines 1/2" apart on a piece of 1/4" stock 4 7/8" long. Use the try square as a guide. Locate the first line 1/2" from one end, which will be the lower end of the ladder. Saw off four strips 1/4" wide.

16. In the center of each line drill a hole about 1/8" deep. A no. 29 drill is just right for a 1/8" rung.

17. Put glue on the ends of each rung and insert them into one rail.

18. Again apply glue and insert the rungs into the other rail.

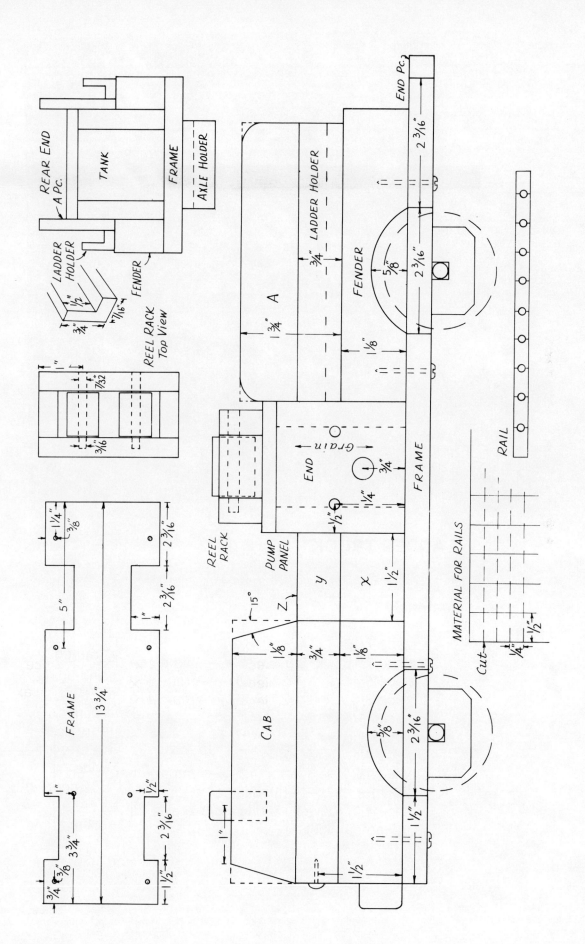

REAR END
A Pc.

TANK

FRAME

AXLE HOLDER

LADDER HOLDER
1/2"
3/4"
7/16"
FENDER

REEL RACK
Top View

1"
7/32"
3/16"

FRAME
13 3/4"
5"
1 1/4"
3/8"
2 3/16"
1"
2 3/16"
3/4"
3 3/4"
3/8"
1"
1/2"
2 3/16"
1/2"

A
1 3/4"

3/4" LADDER HOLDER

FENDER
5/8"
2 3/16"
1 1/8"

REEL RACK

PUMP
PANEL

END
Grain
3/4"
1/2"
1/4"

FRAME

y
x
Z
15°
1 1/8"
3/4"
1 1/8"
1 1/2"

CAB
5/8"
2 3/16"
1"
1 1/2"
1/2"

MATERIAL FOR RAILS
Cut
1/4"
1/2"

RAIL

End Pc.
2 3/16"

171

LADDER TRUCK

Materials

1 piece 7/16″ × 4″ × 16 1/2″ ⎫
1 piece 7/16″ × 3/8″ × 4″——end piece ⎬ frame

1 piece 3/4″ × 1 1/2″ × 3″——front ⎫
1 piece 3/4″ × 1 1/2″ × 2″——rear ⎬ axle holders

2 pieces 1/4″ dowel 4 1/4″ long——axles

2 pieces 1/8″ × 4″ × 4 1/2″ ⎫
1 piece 3/4″ × 4″ × 4 1/2″
1 piece 1/2″ × 3/4″ × 4″——bumper—hardwood ⎬ cab
4 furniture nails——headlights
1 piece 1/2″ dowel 1″ long (or use axle pin)——
    warning light

172

```
1 piece 3/4" × 3 15/16" × 4 3/8"——platform  ⎫
2 pieces 3/4" × 1 1/8" × 4 3/8"——supports   ⎪
1 piece 1 1/8" × 1" × 1 1/4"——ladder holder ⎪ turntable
1 piece 1/2" dowel 2 1/4" long              ⎬ assembly
1    3 1/2" disc 7/16" thick——turntable     ⎪
1    2" disc 7/16" thick                     ⎪
1    1 1/4" fender washer                    ⎭
1 no. 6 round-or pan-head screw
2 pieces 1 1/8" × 1 1/2" × 6"——fenders
1 piece 7/16" × 3" × 8"——deck               ⎫
2 pieces 3/8" × 1 1/8" × 8"——sides          ⎬ ladder cradle
2 pieces 5/8" × 3/4" × 4"——supports         ⎭
2 pieces 3/4" × 3/4" × 1 3/4"——small ladder supports
2 pieces 3/8" × 1/2" × 15"——rails—          ⎫
   hardwood                                  ⎬ main ladder
28 pieces 1/8" dowels 1 5/8" long——rungs    ⎭
2 pieces 5/16" × 5/16" × 9"——rails—hardwood ⎫ small ladder
17 pieces 1/8" dowel 7/8" long——rungs        ⎭
12 no. 6    1" pan-or round-head screws
6    2" wheels
```

Construction

1. In the frame cut openings for the wheel wells. The front wells are 1 1/2" from the end, 1/2" deep, and 2 3/16" wide. The rear wells are 3 1/2" from the end, 1" deep, and 2 3/16" wide. In the underside of the frame drill 10 holes for the screws (see diagram).

2. Shape the axle holders (see page 7). In the center of each cut a groove lengthwise 9/32" × 9/32". Glue the holders to the frame so that the center of the grooves are in the center of the wheel wells.

3. Glue the end piece to the back of the frame.

4. Set the saw at 15 degrees and saw off both ends of one of the 1 1/8" pieces for the cab. Glue the three pieces together

173

with the 3/4″ piece in the middle. In the top drill a hole 1″ from the front edge and centered for the warning light. With a 2 1/2″ Forstner or Greenlee type bit cut an arc in each side of the cab 1/2″ deep and 1 1/2″ from the front end. The top edge of the arc should be up 5/8″ from the lower edge of the cab. Drive in the headlights 3/8″ and 7/8″ from the side edges and 1 1/2″ from the lower edge. Glue the bumper to the cab even with the lower edge. Glue the cab to the frame even with the front end.

5. Through the center of the turntable platform drill a hole slightly larger than 1/2″. Glue the supports to the platform. In the center of the ladder holder drill a 1/2″ hole 3/4″ deep. Glue the 1/2″ dowel in this hole. Also drill a pilot hole for the 1″ screws in each end 1/2″ from the upper edge and centered.

6. In each disc drill a 1/2″ hole through the center.

7. Apply glue to the underside of the ladder holder and insert the dowel down through the hole in the 3 1/2″ disc. A dowel peg may be put up through the disc into the holder to insure that the holder does not come loose. In the center of the lower end of the dowel drill a pilot hole for the 1″ screw. Put the dowel down through the hole in the platform. Put the 2″ disc on the dowel, then the fender washer, and drive the screw into the dowel. A small washer may be needed if the hole in the fender washer is larger than the head of the screw.

8. Glue the turntable assembly to the frame and against the cab.

9. In each rear fender, using the Forstner or Greenlee type bit, cut an arc 1″ deep in the 1 1/2″ side 1 5/16″ from the front end. Or, place the fenders on the frame above the wheel wells and mark the location of the arc to make sure it is over the well. The top edge of the arc should be up 5/8″ from the lower edge of the fender. Glue the fenders to the frame and against the platform.

10. Glue the small ladder supports to the frame between the fenders even with the front and rear ends of the fenders.

11. Glue the ladder cradle supports to the upper side of the fenders even with the ends. The 3/4″ sides should be on the fenders.

12. Round off two upper corners of the sides of the ladder cradle. Glue the sides to the deck and the cradle to the supports. It will extend about 1 3/4″ at the back.

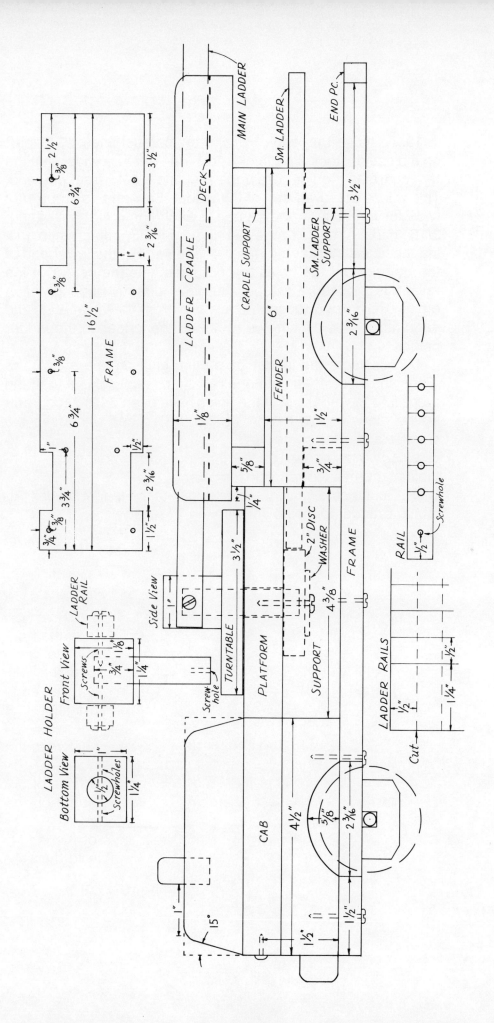

FRAME

2½"
³⁄₈"
6¾"
3½"
2³⁄₁₆"
1"
³⁄₈"
16½"
³⁄₈"
6¾"
³⁄₈"
1"
½"
3¾"
2³⁄₁₆"
1½"
³⁄₄" ³⁄₈"

LADDER CRADLE
DECK
MAIN LADDER
CRADLE SUPPORT
SM. LADDER
SM. LADDER SUPPORT
END PC.
FENDER
6"
3½"
1⅛"
1½"
2³⁄₁₆"
5⁄₈"
³⁄₄"
¼"

LADDER HOLDER
Front View
LADDER RAIL
Screws
¾"
1⅛"
¼"
Bottom View
1"
½"
Screwholes
¼"

Side View
1"
TURNTABLE
PLATFORM
3½"
Screw hole
2" DISC
WASHER
SUPPORT
4³⁄₈"
FRAME

RAIL
Screwhole
½"

LADDER RAILS
½"
1¼"
½"
Cut

CAB
4½"
5⁄₈"
2³⁄₁₆"
15°
1"
1½"
1½"

175

13. To make the ladder rails, draw parallel lines 1/2" apart on a piece of stock 3/8" thick and 1 1/8" or more wide. Use the try square as a guide. Draw the first line 1 1/4" from one end. This will be the lower end of the ladder. Saw off two strips 1/2" wide for the rails. In the center of each line drill a hole about 3/16" deep. A no. 29 drill is just right for a 1/8" rung. When drilling the holes, start at the top of one rail and at the lower end of the other rail. If the holes are not exactly in the center of the rails, this procedure will put the holes directly opposite each other. Drill holes through the rails 1/2" from the lower ends and centered for the 1" screws to fasten the ladder to the ladder holder.

14. Assemble the ladder by putting glue on one end of the rungs and insert them into one rail. Again apply glue and fit the rungs into the other rail. If the holes have been drilled accurately, the rungs should readily fit into the second rail. Make the smaller ladder the same way.

15. Drive the screws up through the frame into the cab, turntable platform supports, and fenders.

16. Round off slightly the side edges of the ladder holder. Attach the ladder to the holder with the 1" screws.

POLICE CAR

Materials

3 pieces 3/4″ × 1 1/4″ × 7″——body
1 piece 3/4″ × 2 3/16″ × 3 1/2″——roof
2 pieces 1/4″ × 3/8″ × 2 1/2″——bumpers——hardwood
2 furniture nails——headlights
1 piece 1/4″ × 5/8″ × 2″——light holder
2 pieces 3/8″ dowel 5/8″ long——warning lights
1 piece 1/4″ dowel 3/4″ long——siren
2 pieces 1/4″ dowel 2 1/2″ long——axles
4   1 1/4″ wheels

Construction

1. Glue the three body pieces together. Round off the upper edge of both ends of the body and sand.

2. With a 1 1/2″ Greenlee type bit drill the wheel wells to a depth of 3/8″ or the thickness of the wheels being used. Locate the front well 1 1/4″ from the end and the rear well 1 3/4″ from the end. The center of each well should be up 1/4″ from the lower edge. Drill a 9/32″ hole through the center of each well.

3. With the saw set at 40 degrees saw off each end of the roof. Saw along each side edge with the saw set at 5 degrees.

4. Glue the roof to the body about 2 1/4″ from the front end.

5. Drive in the headlights 3/4″ from the lower edge and 1/4″ from the side edges.

6. Glue on the bumpers.

7. In the light holder drill a 3/8″ hole 5/16″ from each end. Across the center of the holder make a groove for the siren. Round off one end (upper) of the warning lights and insert them into the holes. Round off one end of the siren and glue it in the groove.

8. Center the light assembly on the roof and glue in place.

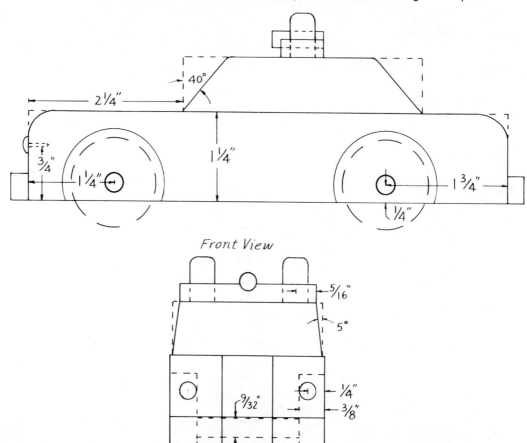

Front View

FIRE CHIEF'S STATION WAGON

Materials

3 pieces 3/4″ × 1 1/4″ × 7″——body
1 piece 3/4″ × 2 3/16″ × 4 3/4″——roof
2 pieces 1/4″ × 3/8″ × 2 1/2″——bumper—hardwood
2 furniture nails——headlights
1 piece 3/8″ dowel 7/8″ long (or use axle pin)——warning
    light
2 pieces 1/4″ dowel 2 1/2″ long——axles
4   1 1/4″ wheels

Construction

1. Glue the three body pieces together. Round off the upper edge of one end (front) and sand.

2. With a 1 1/2″ Greenlee type bit drill the wheel wells to a depth of 3/8″ or the thickness of the wheels being used. Locate the front well 1 1/4″ from the end and the rear well 1 3/4″ from the end. The center of each well should be up 1/4″ from the lower edge. Through the center of each well drill a 9/32″ hole.

3. Saw each end of the roof with the saw tilted at 40 degrees. Saw along each side edge with the saw set at 5 degrees.

4. Glue the roof to the body even with the back end.

5. Drive in the headlights 1/4″ from the side edges and 3/4″ from the lower edge.

6. Glue on the bumpers.

7. Drill a hole for the warning light about 1/2″ deep, 3/4″ back from the front edge of the roof, and centered. Round off one end of the dowel and insert it into the hole.

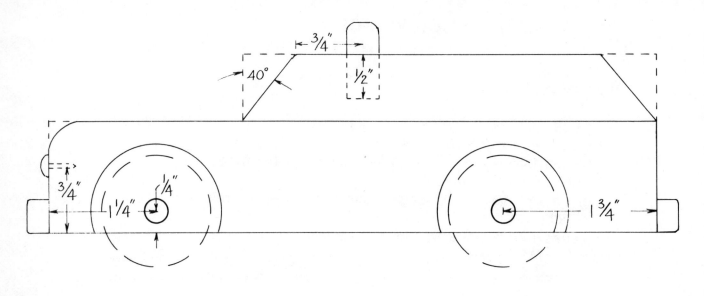

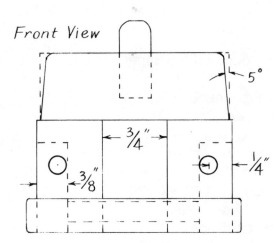

Front View

RACER

Materials

    1 piece 7/16″ × 1 5/16″ × 8″——frame
    3 pieces 7/16″ × 1 1/8″ × 4″——front end
    1 piece 1 1/8″ × 1 5/16″ × 2 1/2″——rear end
    1 piece 1/8″ × 1 5/16″ × 1 1/8″——dashboard—plywood
    1 piece 7/16″ × 3/4″ × 1 5/16″——seat
    1 piece 3/16″ dowel about 1″ long——steering shaft
    1   3/4″ wheel——steering wheel
    8 beads about 1/2″ × 1/2″ (or use 4 beads   1″ long)——
        spacers
    2 pieces 1/4″ dowel 5″ long——axles
    4   1 1/2″ wheels 3/4″ thick

Construction

1. Glue the three front end pieces together. If a wood of a different color, such as redwood, is used for the middle piece, it will add to the appearance of the racer.

2. Drill 9/32″ holes, from side to side, through the frame for the axles. Locate the front hole 1 1/2″ from the end and the rear hole 1″ from the end, and centered.

3. Glue the back piece to the frame even with the end. Round off the top rear end of this piece.

4. Shape the front end. The jig shown with the speed boat (page 125) can be used for this. Sand the upper surface.

5. Glue the dashboard to the rear end of the front piece. Drill a hole slightly larger than 3/16″ through the dashboard into the end about 5/8″ deep for the steering shaft. Locate the hole 5/8″ from the lower edge and centered.

6. Glue the front end to the frame.

7. Glue the steering wheel to the shaft and insert the shaft into the hole.

8. Glue the seat to the frame and against the rear end.

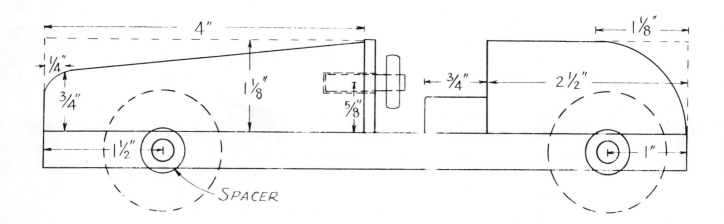

Appendix •
Sources of Supplies and Tools

Tools and other items for the toymaker may be purchased from the following (catalogs are available):

Craftsman Wood Service Company
2727 South Mary Street
Chicago, IL 60608

Woodcraft Supply Corporation
313 Montvale Avenue
Woburn, MA 01801

Brookstone Company
475 Vose Farm Road
Peterborough, NH 03458

Wooden wheels and other supplies can be obtained from the following:

Love-Built Toys and Crafts
2907 Lake Forest Road
P.O. Box 5459
Tahoe City, CA 95730
($1.00 for catalog)

H. G. Winter and Sons
Kingfield, ME 04947
(Minimum quantity per order
15,000–20,000 pieces for
any one item)

Brown Wood Products Company
203 Northfield Road
Northfield, IL 60093
(Minimum order $25.00)

Ebco Inc. (rubber wheels)
6942 West Higgins Avenue
Chicago, IL 60656
($250.00 minimum per order)

Index